The Red Flag Rescue Plan

Recognize, Respond, and Recover from Toxic Relationships

Owen Hadley

Contents

Introduction

Have you ever wondered if your relationship is truly healthy? Are you receiving the love, care, trust and respect that you deserve from your partner? These are important questions to ask ourselves from time to time to ensure our basic needs are being met. Human connection is so vital for our mental well-being and happiness, but not every relationship fulfills this need in a positive way.

In this chapter, we will explore the concept of "red flags" and how to recognize when a relationship may be becoming toxic or damaging to your well-being. As the quote at the beginning mentions, relationships go through ups and downs - no couple is perfect and problems will inevitably arise. However, some relationships cross the line into an unhealthy territory. It's crucial that we learn to identify the warning signs so we don't look back years later wondering why we ignored our gut feelings for so long.

So what exactly constitutes a red flag? At their core, red flags indicate an imbalance of power and control in the relationship. They are behaviors, personality traits or ways of interacting that chip away at your sense of independence, self-esteem and personal boundaries over time. On their own, one or two red flags may seem trivial, but taken together they can diminish your well-being and trap you in an abusive situation. Some common red flags include extreme jealousy, anger issues, blaming you for their mistakes, disrespecting your opinions or isolating you from friends and family.

Have you ever caught yourself walking on eggshells around your partner out of fear of their reaction? Do you feel constantly stressed or anxious in the relationship? These could be signs that the dynamic is becoming unhealthy. Toxic relationships are characterized by a level of harm - whether it be mental, emotional, financial or even physical abuse. Partners in toxic relationships often feel they can't live up to an unrealistic ideal set by the other, and experience controlling behavior aimed at dominating every aspect of their life.

What is a Red Flag?

So what exactly is a red flag? A red flag is a warning sign that something might not be right in a relationship. Red flags indicate potential issues like manipulation, disrespect or other unhealthy behaviors.

Red flags can be subtle at first. They don't always jump out at you right away. Over time, small things can add up and get worse if nothing changes. Common red flags to watch out for include aggression, extreme jealousy or possessiveness, breaking promises, blaming others for their own mistakes, or trying to isolate you from friends and family.

These types of behaviors chip away at trust and respect in a relationship. They slowly diminish the other person's independence and self-esteem. You might start feeling anxious around your partner or walk on eggshells, nervous about their reactions. Red flags make the relationship feel draining rather than bringing you joy and support.

If someone shows early red flags, it's smart to pause and think critically about the relationship. Are both people able to be themselves? Do you feel cared for and that your needs are equally important? Unhealthy behavior often sneaks up gradually, so it's good to look objectively at how the relationship affects your daily life and mood.

Remember, one or two red flags on their own may not mean much. But together over time they can point to deeper problems, especially if nothing changes when you address concerns. Watching closely for repeated red flags helps spot manipulation or abuse early before it damages your well-being. Overall, your happiness and safety should be the top priority in any relationship.

When and How Red Flags Arise

So when do red flags in relationships first appear? The truth is, unhealthy behaviors can develop at any stage of a relationship. Sometimes red flags are evident right from the beginning, while other times things seem fine at first but slowly change over months or years. It's important to realize that relationships are dynamic - as people and circumstances evolve, so too can behaviors and warning signs.

In the early stages of dating, also called the "honeymoon phase", both partners are often on their best behavior. Problems may be less visible as two people get to know each other. However, Jean notices her new boyfriend becomes possessive if she talks to other men. This type of early red flag for abuse or manipulation should not be ignored.

More often though, red flags tend to surface later after the initial infatuation wears off. As intimacy and comfort grow in a relationship, some people feel able to drop their guard and act out frustrations in unhealthy ways. Perhaps Sarah's partner hasn't changed jobs in two years due to laziness, but she overlooks this at first, hoping things will improve. Over time, his excuses start wearing her down.

Occasionally, what seemed like a considerate and supportive partner transforms into someone else completely as months or years pass. Close friends note subtler signs of control or hostility developing that the abused partner misses due to living in the situation daily. As abusive individuals perceive less risk of consequences, restraints on their behavior may weaken.

Abusers often prey on victim's trusting nature and willingness to see the good in people. The change from loving to harmful is gradual to avoid detection. By the time physical abuse occurs, the abused partner's self-esteem has been broken down through other red flags like insults or isolation. Leaving feels impossible in this state of confusion and fear.

Being alert to how red flags may develop over time is key to avoiding or escaping unhealthy relationships before serious damage occurs. No one should accept erosion of their well-being or dignity due to another's poor actions.

Why We Ignore Red Flags

So if red flags can indicate potential problems in a relationship, why do we sometimes fail to notice or acknowledge them? There are a few key reasons why red flags may be ignored or minimized.

In the early stages of a new romance, it's natural to see someone in an idealized light. We focus more on the positive qualities we're attracted to and overlook potential flaws. This "honeymoon phase" sweeps us up in strong feelings that can cloud our judgment. Behaviors that would normally raise concerns get rationalized away.

Manipulative partners also intentionally "love bomb" us with non-stop compliments, gifts and attention to gain control. This overwhelming affection triggers powerful brain chemicals that we crave. It's easy to feel addicted to such intense validation and excuse increasingly possessive tactics to keep it coming.

Once invested emotionally in someone, our natural tendency is to see the good in them and hope issues can be worked through. Admitting red flags may destroy the vision of our "perfect" relationship. We don't want to believe the person we care for could harm us. It's more comfortable trusting things will improve if we're understanding or patient enough.

We also have a bias to remember the positive shared experiences that attracted us to our partner in the first place. Negative patterns get reinterpreted to preserve that initial vision. However, ignoring signs of toxicity allows problems to strengthen their hold over time.

Relationships ebb and flow naturally through ups and downs too. It's human to want to believe challenges can be overcome through love and effort alone. But some behavioral traits fundamentally undermine healthy dynamics if left unaddressed respectfully.

Seeking outside perspectives may help combat these rationalizations. Close friends with our best interests at heart can notice subtle disrespect or control that blurs for those living it day to day. Their removal provides clarity on concerning behaviors versus harmless quirks.

The Health Consequences of Toxicity

So we've discussed red flags to watch out for in a partner's words and actions. But it's also important to tune in to how the relationship makes you feel emotionally and physically. The longer toxicity goes unchecked, the worse health problems can become. Paying attention to our inner experience gives valuable clues to how a bond truly affects well-being.

If constant stress from a relationship disrupts sleep, it shows the mind and body are diverting resources to coping that could be spent recovering. Over time, lack of rest can seriously impact the immune system and lead to further issues. Often people in toxic situations also feel emotionally drained all the time, like walking on eggshells to avoid upsetting their partner. Feeling guilty, ashamed or fearful regularly is mentally and spiritually draining.

Toxic relationships are also commonly linked to physical symptoms since stress reactions are deeply rooted in biology. Many people experience tightness in the chest, high blood pressure, digestive problems and headaches as their body constantly braces for difficulties. If these somatic complaints arise frequently tied to relationship interactions, it signals unhealthy dynamics are taking a toll.

Dreading time together or withholding honesty to preemptively control explosions from a partner are also red flags. Healthy bonds make people excited to share life, not dreading contact. We intuitively protect ourselves from predictable harms, so these feelings could reflect necessary boundaries being crossed on a regular basis.

Overall, pay attention if a relationship leaves you feeling constantly unhappy, anxious or depleted versus energized and able to fully be yourself. While compromise is normal, toxicity predictably chips away at wellness over months and years if roots of problems remain unresolved. If inner experience indicates it's time for difficult conversations or separation, make caring for your whole self the priority with support from trusted loved ones. You deserve to thrive in relationships, not just survive.

Recognizing Toxic Behavior

We've all walked away from an interaction feeling stressed, irritated or like something just wasn't right. These are likely when you encountered someone exhibiting toxic behavior without even realizing it. These difficult people have a way of subtly throwing us off our game and leaving us second-guessing ourselves if we're not careful.

Toxic people come in every shape and form. It could be a coworker who avoids honest communication, creating distrust. Perhaps a friend who's constantly negative and finds fault in everything. Or maybe it's a critical family member who shirks responsibility and blames others. Their tactics vary too - some are outright hostile while others operate more covertly through passive-aggression.

So how can we identify these troublesome behaviors early before they start to negatively impact our well-being? The first step is understanding how toxicity typically presents itself.

In many cases, problematic conduct is pretty straightforward to spot. An overly hostile boss who's never satisfied or an uncooperative team member leaving you with all the work are good examples. But toxic behavior isn't always so glaringly obvious. Sometimes the issues are more subtle, like that one coworker who always seems to nitpick your ideas in meetings. Or the friend who never seems genuinely excited when you share your news. You start to feel constantly undermined or let down without knowing why.

Trust your instincts in these ambiguous situations. What bugs you in one context may be a non-issue in another. For example, you might be able to easily shrug off your teenager's mocking jokes but have zero tolerance for similar behavior from your manager.

Toxicity exists on a spectrum too. On one end are overtly problematic folks - hostile, aggressive and blatantly difficult to deal with. On the other side are more passive types who are uninvolved and uncaring. Their behavior is irritating in different ways.

But it's often the behaviors somewhere in the middle that are the most perplexing - things like passive-aggression. These covert, dishonest manipulations leave you perplexed about exactly what's causing the frustration.

When does someone cross the line from mildly irritating to a full-blown toxic person? It's usually a slow progression going from small behaviors that they aren't called out on. What at first seems like a minor annoyance can escalate into significant toxicity if allowed to continue unchecked.

Pay attention to how interactions make you feel over time. Do you frequently leave dialogues feeling stressed, disrespected or like the other person was being deliberately obtuse? Are there patterns of you feeling constantly put-down, criticized or flustered without good reason?

These are red flags that indicate potentially problematic behavior. It's so important to recognize them early before we start questioning our own perceptions or acting out of character. That's when toxicity has started taking its toll. Once you can spot the signs, it becomes easier to address issues respectfully while also taking back your power. In later sections, we'll explore specific behaviors to watch out for and strategies for navigating difficult situations with poise.

Openly Hostile and Aggressive Behavior

If you ever encounter someone who starts shouting, swearing, or putting you down during a meeting or gathering you may feel intimidated. You shut down from their harsh and forceful behavior, feeling intimidated. This is aggressive behavior. As we've discussed, toxic behaviors exist on a spectrum. At one end are those who actively try to intimidate and control through outright aggression and hostility. Learning to identify these tactics is an important part of safeguarding your well-being.

Overt Displays of Anger

Some clear signs of openly hostile behavior include loud shouting or swearing, even over minor issues. The person takes disagreements very personally and sees any alternative views as a direct attack. They speak over others in conversations and are completely rigid in their stances, believing compromise is foolish. Criticism of any kind seems to trigger disproportionate anger.

But why do some individuals exhibit such aggression? At their core, it often stems from deep insecurity and an inability to handle not getting their way. When expectations are contradicted or their authority is questioned in any way, it activates feelings of vulnerability. Not wanting to appear weak, the easy path becomes rage and attempts to domineer the situation through volume and forcefulness.

Of course, lived experiences also play a role. People who grew up in volatile homes may struggle to process emotions healthily as adults. Constantly walking on eggshells teaches the language of threat over the language of understanding. Without learning healthier coping mechanisms, lashing out becomes second nature in challenging times

Anger vs. Aggression

It's useful to distinguish between anger, an emotional state, and aggression, the outward behavior. Getting angry is normal and sometimes warranted. However, not all anger needs an aggressive outlet. Some channel irritation constructively through conversation while others react impulsively through intimidation and confrontation.

Two main aggressive styles include instrumental aggression used deliberately to manipulate outcomes, and impulsive aggression as an automatically defensive response to perceived threats. The former is more calculated while the latter stems from inability to self-regulate during emotional flashes.

Those employing instrumental hostility have learned aggression can terrify others into submission. Through domineering tactics like shouting over others, they avoid real engagement and silencing alternative stances. This maintains the illusion of always being right to satisfy their bruised egos.

The goal is establishing control and getting what they want at any cost. Compromise threatens that authority so it's viewed as weakness. Unfortunately, coercive behaviors often temporarily accomplish their aims through fear rather than respect or understanding.

When dealing with openly hostile individuals, protecting yourself should be top priority. Removing yourself from escalating situations if possible is sometimes the wisest strategy, as anger can cloud rational thinking. Engaging may just fuel further volatility if the person feels profoundly threatened or refuses self-reflection.

If you do opt to address their conduct, do so with confidence, composure and respect for your own boundaries. Present facts calmly without reactionary insults that may provoke more conflict. Leaving interactions in control of your emotional response denies their desire to manipulate you.

Overall, prioritize disengaging peacefully whenever needed for safety. Toxicity aims to provoke strong reactions for fuel, so respond strategically rather than give into fear-based instincts. With self-awareness comes power over how such challenges affect your well-being.

Navigating Disguised Hostility

You know that feeling, don't you? When someone's words and actions don't quite align, leaving you utterly confused and questioning your own reality. Welcome to the world of passive aggression – a realm where hostility is cloaked in ambiguity and veiled beneath a seemingly passive exterior.

Openly hostile behavior is unmistakable, an in-your-face display of aggression. But passive aggression? That's a different beast entirely. It's an indirect expression of what someone truly wants (or doesn't want), conveyed through obscure, underhanded tactics that leave you tying yourself in knots, trying to decipher the hidden motives.

Decoding the Language of Passive Aggression

When dealing with passive aggressive individuals, you'll quickly notice their penchant for mixed messages and sarcastic, veiled jabs. They'll say one thing but mean another, often following up with a dismissive "just kidding" or accusing you of overreacting when you rightfully take offense.

Instead of articulating their thoughts and feelings directly, these individuals might mutter their dissent under their breath, roll their eyes, or give you the infamous silent treatment or dirty looks. They're masters of the victim mentality, unwilling to take responsibility for their actions and emotions, which they often bring upon themselves through their own manipulative behavior.

Actions Speak Louder Than Words

Passive aggression isn't limited to verbal cues; it manifests in actions as well. At work or home, these individuals might appear cooperative on the surface, but their actions tell a different story. They'll disrupt tasks, sabotage projects, or create confusion, all the while claiming ignorance or innocence.

They'll decline to contribute ideas, only to smugly proclaim, "I knew it wouldn't work," when your efforts falter. Excuses, delays, and procrastination are their weapons of choice, as they stall, drag their heels, and "forget" about their responsibilities. They might even deliberately perform tasks poorly or leave them incomplete, all in the name of resistance.

The Roots of Passive Aggression

So, why do people resort to such underhanded tactics? Often, it stems from a fear of confrontation, hidden anger, or an inability to communicate directly. They might lack the confidence to assert themselves or have been discouraged from openly expressing their feelings in the past, resorting to less detectable methods to convey their thoughts and emotions.

Unlike passive individuals who simply accept the needs and opinions of others, passive aggressive types are unwilling to submit. However, instead of asserting themselves in direct, honest ways, they employ underhanded tactics to get what they want.

Navigating the Minefield of Passive Aggression

Dealing with passive aggression can be a minefield, leaving you feeling confused, upset, offended, or frustrated. You might even start to question yourself, wondering if you've done something wrong (spoiler alert: you likely haven't).

The key to navigating this tricky terrain is to resist the urge to match their passive aggression with overt aggression of your own. Instead, calmly and assertively address the behavior, calling it out for what it is without resorting to hostility yourself.

Remember, passive aggression is a form of conflict that avoids real issues, so engage sensibly and directly. If the person is unwilling or unable to communicate openly, you might need to disengage from the situation, at least temporarily, for the sake of your own well-being.

Ultimately, dealing with passive aggression requires patience, self-awareness, and a commitment to open, honest communication. By understanding the root causes and recognizing the tactics, you can reclaim your power and refuse to be a victim of disguised hostility.

Recognize The Victim Mentality

Some individuals seem to constantly view themselves as put-upon or hard-done-by, bracing for the next injustice no matter how small. They perceive struggle as inevitable and assume misfortune is always looming just around the corner.

This perpetual outlook of hardship is what's known as the victim mentality. People who subscribe to this mindset see themselves as subjects of relentless circumstance beyond their control. No good deed goes unpunished in their eyes, and unfairness is sure to strike again given the chance.

Walking on Eggshells

Interacting with chronic victims means carefully navigating conversations like a mine-field. You feel compelled to consider every word and action, worried the slightest slip may catalyze an outburst accusing you of some slight. Unspoken rules seem ever in flux as triggers change without warning.

It's exhausting tiptoeing this way, braced for the next hair-trigger reaction. Their sensitivity governs all interactions to an draining extent. Any hint of rejection, no matter how minor, activates hostility just under the surface ready to erupt.

A Self-Fulfilling Prophecy

Ironically, constant negativity and readiness for misfortune often becomes a self-ful-filling prophecy. Over time, perpetual victimhood repels potential sources of support. When interactions feel like emotional hostage situations, others learn to avoid or disengage.

This reinforcement of isolation perpetuates the victim's feelings of injustice. They use growing loneliness to "prove" the world conspires only to let them down. No room remains for personal responsibility in the narrative, only further proof that life subjects them to inequality.

Sympathy and Self-Pity

Some gravitate to victimization due its allure as a crutch. It feels addictive and com-forting to wallow melodramatically in one's struggles, seeking sympathy through tales of unfair deprivation. They exact a tax of emotional labor, demanding you understand the immense depths of their suffering above all else.

Validation becomes the goal over solutions. Accepting self-determination would relin-quish the victim label, so responsibility gets shirked and problems externalized without end. Life keeps "doing this" to them regardless of choices or circumstances in their control.

Breaking Free

Escaping this mentality requires determination and patience. First understand its roots through compassionate listening absent judgment. Then gently challenge unhelpful thinking by encouraging accountability, focus on present solutions rather than past hurts, and remind that perceived injustice alone won't dictate your quality of life.

Most importantly, willingly break the self-perpetuating cycle by accepting you determine your reactions and outlook, not others or past events. With practice emphasizing strengths over limitations, you trade victimhood for empowerment through an active, not reactive spirit.

It's a learning process that takes courage. But mental freedom and authentic relationships become well worth regaining control of your narrative instead of surrendering to a mindset based in helplessness. The rewards of empowerment far surpass those of perceived victimization.

The Negative Mindset

The lens through which we view the world profoundly shapes our experiences and interactions. Those who subscribe to negative thought patterns tend to see opportunities as obstacles and possibilities as perpetual downfalls waiting to unfold. Their bleak outlook becomes a self-fulfilling prophecy, often detracting from their own lives as much as the lives of others.

However, perspective is not pre-determined but a choice - we each hold power over the narratives we create. While negativity may seem ingrained, its grip can be loosened by cultivating resilience through empowered mindsets. Focusing outward on controlling externalities less and inward on personalized growth more allows escaping toxicity's reach.

Emotional Vampirism

Those mired in negativity drain positivity from discussions. Minor hurdles morph catastrophically in their retellings, leaving no room for potential upsides. Like vampires thirsting after emotional energy, their sole focus seems fueling doom scenarios at the cost of others' morale. Attempting to spread gloom becomes an addiction all its own, filling some void through the company of spreading pessimism.

But we each guard stewardship over our attitudes and how they influence connections. While negativity spreads easily when left unaddressed, recognizing its tactics arms you to avoid internalizing bleakness. You need not entertain those fixated on dismantling hope to feel validated. Prioritizing circles uplifting your spirit nourishes well-being over darker company.

The Contagion Effect

If negativity goes unchallenged long enough, its distorted perceptions seep into normalizing limited beliefs even regarding yourself. Those chronically projecting doubt onto others' aspirations eventually direct such skepticism inward too if you permit it.

Your potential becomes distorted through their filter of inevitable failure absent resistance. Where you see opportunities, their version of you foresee only inadequacy and confirms their distrust. If this warped reflection replaces your authentic self-image, their toxicity succeeds in its mission to deflate resilience wherever it goes.

Breaking Free

Acknowledge negativity's effect yet refuse defining yourself through another's narrowed lens. When its distorted perceptions creep into your thoughts, actively challenge unhelpful assumptions through counter-evidence and reframing.

Focus on nurturing support systems uplifting potential instead of tearing it down. Make empowering self-talk a daily habit contrasting negatives' rhetoric. Frame difficulties as lessons propelling growth, not roadblocks of doom. With practice, you condition resilience rejecting toxicity's pull in favor of authentic self-belief.

The Power of Optimism

Optimism does not blind itself to reality but empower confronting it. This mindset cultivates ability to transform hardship into strength, problems into solutions, and setbacks into launching pads for greater heights.

It replaces distrust with faith in overcoming through flexible thinking and community. Optimism attracts auspicious circumstances whereas negativity becomes a self-sabotaging destiny. You free yourself catalyzing positive change by shifting internal monologue from limitations to opportunities underlying any situation.

With this shift comes immunity to the doubt of others no matter how ceaseless. Nothing holds you back from pursuing dreams and lifting both yourself and those around you in the process. Darkness resides only where light does not enter; bring sunlight and dispel gloom wherever your journey leads.

Understanding Passive Behavior

Some individuals have mastered the art of disengagement, blending seamlessly into surroundings and interactions by bearing little of their true selves. Always ready with an agreeable attitude yet reticent to impose views, these are the hallmarks of a passive personality. By avoiding standing out in any way, they believe they minimize potential for disapproval or friction.

However, this compliance comes at the cost of authenticity. Over time, constant retreat into acquiescence obscures one's genuine identity, values and needs. These are instead subordinated in favor of appearing cooperative above all else. While seeming harmonious, such detachment grows dissatisfying for all involved as true involvement remains elusive.

Varied Faces of Passivity

Passive tendencies take various shapes. In some, you see embodied the friend without strong opinions, content echoing others' preferences. Others present as the coworker who rarely declines additional duties yet consistently underdelivers, unable directly assert realistic limitations.

Then there are sidelines lingerers, disengaged and removed from meaningful participation yet unlikely confrontational. Their avoidant natures foster assumptions of tranquility while quietly festering resentment at perpetual autonomy deprivation. At first, nonresistance seems respite but soon frustrates as true investment proves superficial.

Listening for Retreat

Pay heed also to the language of withdrawal. Phrases signaling evasion like "I don't mind", "Whatever you think", "It's up to you" ooze from mouths seeking refuge in indecision over vulnerability. Prolonged deflection leaves others unclear on depths of care for issues, let alone true inclinations.

Concerns remain unvalidated through disinterest in supporting stances hesitantly taken. Reluctance to ever counter or affirm leaves relations feeling one-sided and aloof despite surface-level harmony. These habits incite suspicion over authentic willingness to engage on meaningful levels.

Roots of the Agreeable Mask

Driving some into passivity lie childhoods where self-expression invited censure. They normalized fading into backgrounds as means avoiding disapproval. Others fear disruption to likeable façades, convinced needs asserted jeopardize regard. Still more simply can't muster investment in dynamic worlds passing them by anonymously.

Whatever roots, passivity constricts fulfillment for self and community. While appearing affable, prolonged reticence to participate authentically sows discontent where true knowing might bloom. Relations remain unsatisfying for all where potential remains untapped.

Reclaiming Presence

Acknowledging disengagement allows intent focus on progression. Small acts gradually practicing forthrightness cultivate comfort in worth of individuality. Seeking encouragement instead of performance-based validation empowers emergence from shells.

When convenient compliance beckons, pause interrogating authentic inclinations. Assert needs firmly yet respectfully. With dedication to owning truth despite temptation appeasing at its cost, presence revives where once faded. Liberated expression fosters integrity and nourishes bonds affirming value beyond surface harmony.

Steadfast commitment to this work liberates all from passivity's muted control. Regained authenticity activates community and self-realization in place of obscurity serving no one well. Each step reawakens involvement wherever withdrawn, restoring integrity and potential wherever passively withheld.

The Cycle of Toxicity

Alright friends, this is an important topic we're discussing today. Dealing with toxic people and unhealthy relationships can really wear us down if we don't take steps to address it. I know from personal experience just how draining it can feel to constantly question yourself or feel like you're walking on eggshells around certain folks. But have no fear - by educating ourselves on these issues and using practical strategies, we have the power to reshape those dynamics and take back control of our own well-being.

The "cycle of toxicity" is a phrase I've found really helpful in making sense of situations that left me feeling stuck and confused. Essentially what happens is relationships with toxic traits tend to follow a predictable pattern that keeps us hooked in, even when deep down we know it's not serving us well. It starts with a "love bombing" phase where the other person showers us with attention, compliments, gifts, promises - you name it. We feel special and cared for. But before long, thatintensity fades and things take a turn. Criticisms start, boundaries get pushed,gaslighting and guilt trips ensue. We're left feeling off balance, unsure ifwe're imagining things. If we try to set limits, the loving phase resumesjust long enough to draw us back in. Sound familiar to any of you?

I think what's key to understand is that cycle thrives on unpredictability and control. When someone routinely abandons kindness only to suddenly shower uswith affection again, our reactions get conditioned. It breaks down our natural defenses so we doubt our perceptions and prioritize pleasing them overour own well-being. Has anyone else noticed how exhausting it becomes tryingso desperately to anticipate the other person's shifting moods or figure outwhat "set them off" this time? We lose ourselves in the process.

The good news is merely recognizing that cycle exists is a giant step already towards healing. It means we can stop blaming ourselves when things flip-flop,knowing it's a purposeful manipulation tactic, not a flaw within us. We regain our confidence in trusting our own judgments and experiences. From there, we need to take practical steps like distancing ourselves from the toxic individual, focusing on supportive relationships instead, and finding healthier outlets for our time and energy like hobbies, exercise or counseling. It's also critical not to get pulled back in even when they inevitably come around saying just the right things to stir up that familiar hope and comfort again. We know where that leads, don't we?

To help you lift the fog and clearly understand how toxicity perpetuates, here's how it normally goes:

Phase 1: Tension Building

The tension building phase is often when the seeds of doubt are first planted in our minds. We start to notice tiny shifts in the way our partner interacts with us that leaves us feeling slightly unsettled, though it can be hard to pinpoint exactly why. Their words may take on a new sharpness at times, or they get irritated more easily by little things we say or do. Looking back, I can remember times I walked on eggshells, censoring myself carefully so as not to do anything that could trigger the volatile moods I sensed were brewing just beneath the surface.

It really is like living with storm clouds that are darkening by the day. You know a downpour is coming but there's no telling when the skies will finally open up. This constant state of uneasy limbo is exhausting to endure. I found myself constantly analyzing every look and comment for clues, desperate to understand what I'd done wrong so I could fix it preemptively. But the truth is, their frustration often wasn't really about me or anything I'd done - it was about power and control.

During tension building, even neutral discussions could suddenly escalate into full blown arguments. If I tried to explain my perspective, I'd be talked over or have my words twisted until I wasn't sure what was being discussed anymore. It felt hopeless, like we were going in endless circles. Easier to retreat into silence, though that only provided temporary relief. Being on edge for so long really starts to take a toll on your mental health too. You constantly feel like you're walking an invisible tightrope and one wrong move could trigger the explosion you dread. It's psychologically draining.

For some, the tension might show itself through more overt aggression like yelling or physical intimidation tactics. But manipulation can also be subtler, like the silent treatment, insults disguised as jokes or pretending things you said were "misunderstood" when really, the goal is confusion. The fear of that next outburst has you constantly adjusting to keep them placated. Over time, this erosion of boundaries and self-worth is how abusers gain such a stronghold over their victims. We lose our own identity.

Recognizing these patterns for what they are - tactics to destabilize and control - is such a empowering realization. It removes their power to distort reality and put the responsibility back on their own unhealthy behavior where it belongs. Once the fog starts to clear, you can make choices free of their gaslighting like confiding in a supportive network, documenting incidents or starting to rebuild your independence. No one deserves to feel like they're treading on eggshells in their own home or relationship. You've got this - trust your intuition and remember your worth. Brighter days are ahead.

Phase 2: The Incident

The incident phase is undoubtedly the most frightening part of the cycle to experience firsthand. Up until that point, the tension and power plays may have seemed confusing but not outright dangerous. Then suddenly, like a pressure valve blowing, chaos and harm erupt without warning. It's a truly jarring shift that leaves us reeling, desperately trying to make sense of the unthinkable thing that just transpired between people who were supposed to find comfort in one another.

More than anything, these outbursts aim to devastate our sense of stability and normalize such toxicity. Physical attacks naturally incite tremendous fear, but even seemingly "calmer" incidents like threats or emotional cruelty succeed in chipping away at our boundaries until we aren't sure which way is up. And the whiplash between that chaos and what comes after is almost worse - love bombing serves to deepen the confusion over whether any abuse occurred at all. "They bought me flowers, so it couldn't have been that bad" is a common thought, yet it obscures reality further.

In the wake of incidents, our mind clutches at straws seeking logic where there is none to be found. We question endlessly what we could've done differently to divert their rage, as if we held the magic power to control another's mental health and behavior. But toxic individuals thrive on this very dependence. Threatening the foundation of our relationships and gaslighting us into responsibility for their actions is how they establish a constant power imbalance. It reinforces the notion that walking on eggshells is our only means of peace.

It can be so isolating during this phase because the loving person you knew seems to have vanished without a trace, replaced by a volatile stranger. Who will believe that about someone who always appears so polite and normal to outsiders? This is by design - hiding in plain sight is crucial to continuation of the cycle. Unless we make the conscious decision to accept reality instead of the fantasy they peddle, it will only end in deeper hurt.

Understanding that none of us deserve abuse and that these incidents aim to gain compliance, not correct faults, is liberating truth. It allows us to place responsibility rightfully on the toxic actions instead of with imagined flaws within ourselves. From there, seeking community and safely distancing little by little is the wise path forward. You have so much courage; keep trusting your inner strength even when it's hardest.

Phase 3: Reconciliation

The reconciliation stage can be one of the most hopeful-feeling parts of the cycle, yet also where manipulation runs deepest. After the storm of an incident finally passes, the sun returns with warm assurances that it's now safe to come out of hiding. Sincere apologies and eager promises that "this time will be different" flood in, along with gifts meant to wash away memories of what came before. Amidst this flurry of affection, it's all too easy to get swept up in believing the nightmare is truly over.

I know from personal experience just how seductive that hope is when you're longing to trust someone again. All the logic that this pattern will likely repeat vanishes in favor of enthusiastically accepting their pleas for a fresh start. But real, meaningful change takes continuous effort over time - not just surface-level sweets and speeches. Abusers understand we crave resolution, so they dangle it like bait before disappearing again into old behaviors. The temporary placation obscures that no healing has truly begun.

It's so crucial not to fall for hollow words alone during reconciliation. Watch carefully for concrete actions like pursuing counseling or support groups to gain insight on un-healthy actions. Offer forgiveness tentatively instead of fully, while still guarding yourself. True care demands consistency, not fleeting romance. If past trauma starts bubbling up again too soon, that speaks volumes.

Learning to spot manipulation even in feel-good gestures takes practice but boosts our ability to break cycles. No amount of gifts can make up for damage done to our sense of safety or trust. We must believe we deserve more than a relationship of constant ups and downs wrought by another's moods. Calm today does not guarantee calm tomorrow without real accountability and change.

Ultimately, focusing on empowering ourselves by establishing boundaries, seeking community and activities that nourish well-being independent of others is key. In this way, manipulative tactics lose their power over us. We recognize our intrinsic worth cannot be defined through another's approval

Phase 4: Calm Before the Next Storm

After the turbulence of past incidents, finding ourselves in a tranquil moment with our abuser can stir equal parts relief and dread. On one hand, it's a welcome change to simply enjoy each other's company without constant edge or conflict. Laughter and inside jokes return as that person tries winsomely to convince us they've shifted for good this time. Who wouldn't longing to go back to happier memories of what first drew us to them?

Yet the recognition remains that this soothing interlude is just the eye of another impending storm. No matter how sincere their sentiments may feel in the moment, history proves their behavior modification is fleeting at best before fear and frustration inevitably resurface. At the core, this is not a partner committed to the rigorous personal transformation needed to overcome toxic patterns, but rather an abuser employing a brief pleasantry as misdirection.

It is a privilege, then, to see this deceptive calm for the manipulation it is - not a sign that we were mistaken in past perceptions, but of how sophisticated the techniques to undermine our judgment become. In easier times, we must double our focus inward to bolster ourselves for what's to come, rather than relax defenses or reopen old wounds. Reach for aid networks cultivated independently of this relationship so needed help exists regardless of their monitoring.

Most crucially, understand you deserve far more than a intermittent oasis in a desert of unpredictability. No matter how heavy the urge to accept pretty words as currency for past hurt, stay rooted in the knowledge that real change demands proof over periods, not surface pleasures. Though breaking addiction to cyclical highs and lows requires immense courage, freedom from them more than compensates the difficulty.

When storms do return as they must, maintain faith in your insightful removal rather than doubting what led you here. Each loving gesture toward self and community strengthens your immunity to manipulative tactics. Now that you understand the "Cycle of Toxicity", let's look at how to respond to Toxicity in the next chapter.

Your Response to Toxicity

Has there ever been someone in your life who just seems to bring out the worst in you? You know the type - no matter how many times you've had the same argument, you can't seem to break the cycle. It's like you're both stuck on repeat, playing your roles to the bitter end every. single. time. Well friends, I'm here to tell you that it doesn't have to be this way. You have the power to change the tune, but it will take courage and commitment to reshape those toxic patterns.

I know how exhausting it can feel to be stuck in a familiar groove with someone, repeatedly getting stuck on the same old notes. But what if I told you there was a way to start fresh - to see the relationship with new eyes and break free of the baggage from your history together? Believe it or not, it all comes down to adopting a beginner's mindset. Ever seen a little kid meet someone for the first time? They approach it with such openness and curiosity, unafraid to just be fully present without judgment. That willingness to shed assumptions and see things anew is exactly what we need to face toxicity with new eyes.

Now you may be thinking "But I've known this person for years! How can I possibly treat it like the first time?" And that's a fair point - familiarly does breed habit. But just because patterns have formed over time doesn't mean they have to define you forever. The beauty of a beginner's mind is that it gives us permission to hit reset, even with people we've long been 'acquainted' with. Of course, retraining your brain won't be easy when ruts have been road deep. That's why it's crucial to have a plan so you can weather the bumps along the way.

Before embracing this fresh outlook, take time to think through potential challenges upfront. What's the worst case scenario if old habits die hard? How will you maintain your resolve when resistance hits? Knowing what you're prepared to accept and having strategies in place empowers you to stay focused on the goal - creating new memories unbound by the past. And it's so important to approach this journey with care, compassion, and understanding for both yourself and the other person. Change takes time, and patience is key.

Adjusting Your Expectations

I'm sure you've been in this situation before - feeling let down by someone close to you and realizing it stems from unmet expectations. Perhaps it's a friend who hasn't followed through as many times as you'd hoped or a family member who continually relies on your support. Whatever the case, these underlying expectations we hold shape our relationships in profound ways.

We've all developed implicit rules about how people "should" act based on our own principles and past experiences. But when reality deviates from our standards, it can stir powerful negative emotions. So where do these expectations come from and how do they impact our bonds? Let's explore.

Our expectations are deeply tied to our personal values - the core beliefs that guide our lives. Values develop unconsciously from environmental, social and personal factors over time. They inform what behaviors we view as appropriate or priorities. For example, if reliability is highly valued, one may expect steadiness from others.

However, not everyone shares our exact hierarchy of values. What's most important to you may not be for someone else through no fault of their own. Each person's priorities differ according to their unique life journey. While this doesn't excuse disrespectful actions, it does help explain perceived inconsistencies through alternative perspectives.

Rigidly clinging to preconceived expectations despite these individual variances often breeds resentment and conflict. When we inflexibly demand others constantly adhere to our standards, it places undue strain on relationships and invites frequent disappointments. People are complex, and no two will perfectly align all the time.

So, how can we better approach this? My friend, it all boils down to recognizing your expectations, their origins, and their influence on your interactions with others. And that is exactly what we will look at in the following section.

Your Values and Expectations

The foundation of our expectations lies within our personal values systems. Values are the core principles that have guided us since childhood based on countless influences. Whether it's honesty, loyalty, or independence, the values we hold shape our worldview in profound ways.

By nature of guiding our lives, values also color what behaviors we deem important or "worthy". Do we value efficiency and decisiveness or flexibility and cooperation? This value hierarchy then informs the expectations we develop, consciously or not, of how people close to us should conduct themselves.

For example, if reliability and commitment to plans are near the top of your value list, you likely expect consistency, punctuality, and follow-through from friends and family. When inevitable deviations occur from this standard, feelings of disappointment or frustration can set in quickly.

However, it's crucial to remember that not everyone shares our exact set of personal values or priorities. What may be vitally important to you could be less so for others through no fault of their own. Each individual is conditioned by a unique blend of environmental and personal experiences over time.

Rather than view differences as character flaws or shortcomings, it's healthier to acknowledge the diversity of human psychology. We are not carbon copies, and individual strengths emerge from varied contexts. Someone more flexible may complement your decisiveness well, for instance.

Recognizing this prevents unfair judgments and resentment when reality diverts from our expectations. Though inevitable, divergences need not incite negative emotions if properly understood as natural outcome of individual humanity. With compassion for such diversities, relationships remain hardy in weathering life's inconsistencies.

The Problem With Inflexible Expectations

Of all the expectation traps to avoid, inflexibility is the surest path to strife. When we hold rigidly fixed notions of how others "should" act without exception, it breeds distress. By making our wellbeing hinge entirely on another aligning perfectly to our standards, we invite disappointment at any deviation, no matter how minor.

Before long, this inflexible mentality transforms us into the one constantly perceiving slights where they may not exist for others. Our burden of unrealistic expectations gets unfairly placed upon them as the sole source of troubles. Relationships suffer under this weight, with resentment and tension sure to penetrate if the status quo remains unchanged.

What's more, behaviors are deeply ingrained over many years of nurture and nature. As individuals, we each develop patterns profoundly shaped by unique experiences since childhood. To expect complete overhaul of engrained traits ignores this reality. Just as it would be unrealistic and counterproductive to force our own total behavior shift, so too with others.

Rather than perceiving mismatches through the narrow lens of our personal preferences, cultivating flexibility and context promotes healthier bonds. Not all view the world identically to us, so acceptance of plausible differences prevents disconnection. For example, if a sibling has relied on parents support their whole life and it provides comfort overall, forcing total alteration to satisfy our own interpretation helps no one.

Relationships thrive not by demanding constant adherence to our rigid personalized standards, but through compassionate recognition of human complexity and imperfection. When space opens for individuality rather than judgment of discrepancies, bonds withstand inevitable deviations with ease. In embracing diversity over uniformity, connections deepen.

Adjusting Your Expectations

Breaking free from the negative cycle of unmet expectations is absolutely possible through cultivating awareness and flexibility. The first step begins with self-reflection - noticing when frustrations arise from within implies underlying rigid expectations.

Pay close attention to moments where thoughts of "Why can't they..." or assumptions of "They should..." enter your mind. These subtle signs indicate unrealistic standards lurking beneath the surface. Once noticed, it's time for evaluation.

Gaining objectivity, question if the expectation truly aligns with practical realities. Are specific contexts, individual traits and inherent imperfections acknowledged? Or are they based more on an idealized vision of how you wish things to be? Personal needs matter, yet relationships require adaptation from all parties.

If upon reflection, certain expectations seem inflexibly fixed rather than reasonably aligned, adjustment is key. But this does not entail compromising core values or principles. Rather, it involves aligning standards to the complex truths of human nature and circumstances at play.

For example, acknowledging we all err at times prevents disappointment over minor faults in others. With understanding as the lens, reactions shift from anger to compassion even in discomfort. Through this shifting view, healthier bonds form resilient to life's inevitable deviations large and small.

Open communication becomes a tool where once conflict arose too. By addressing situations with care, empathy and respect, depth replaces surface reactions. Dialogue reveals new perspectives to further adjust standards or find understanding that prevents past frustrations.

Acceptance and Communication

Adjusting expectations need not equate to resignation or loss of boundaries. True acceptance involves recognizing our inherent individuality - that each person's qualities and constraints naturally differ. By gaining this perspective, empowerment emerges through open communication done respectfully.

Rather than retreat inward with frustrations or lash out in reaction, proactively initiate calm discussion. Explain how certain behaviors impact you while actively listening to understand other views fully. Displaying empathy builds trust for mutual insight where defensiveness once reigned.

Through this dialogue, long held frictions dissolve as each party realizes alternative perspectives and unspoken assumptions. Compassion opens where judgment closed, unveiling compromise that satisfies all. New context may reveal reasonable adjustments to expectations or establishment of boundaries with shared meaning.

Navigating the complex interplay between our values, expectations of others, and their individual realities is an ongoing learning process. But each connection strengthened provides reward much greater than conflicts borne of inflexibility and loneliness.

By cultivating heightened self and social awareness, examining preconceptions for rationality over rigidity, and embracing dialogue as a tool for solutions over division, transformation occurs. Relationships blossom as acceptance of diversity overcomes demand for uniformity, unrealistic perspectives adjust to fit complex realities, and communication guides understanding where friction once strained bonds.

Remember, flexibility does not weaken principles or lose agency. It simply means aligning standards to human truth through respect. In so doing, connections grow ever deeper and more resilient to life's inevitable variations, empowering well-being for all involved. Such is the fruit borne of open yet discerning communication within a framework of mutual care, respect and growth.

The Power of Positive Expectations

Expectations are an innate part of human relationships, whether consciously realized or not. How we view others informs our interactions in subtle yet significant ways. While necessary for navigation, negative or rigid expectations often breed strife where flexibility could foster understanding. Let's explore cultivating a mindset centered around positive expectations instead.

Fixating on narrow, outcome-driven expectations leaves little room for human imperfection and uniquely contextualized realities. We've all experienced frustration from placing unrealistic demands upon loved ones, perhaps expecting a sibling to adhere to our view of appropriate independence levels. But people develop over lifelong experiences beyond our perspective. Inflexibility invites tension where acceptance might relieve it.

The downsides become clear - high expectations dependent on precise behaviors risk resentment when complexity intervenes. Judging others for failing to emulate idealized versions of ourselves corrodes bonds. A more optimistic alternative emerges through embracing diversity of human experience.

Rather than fixating on preconceived ideals, positive expectations focus on the overall growth and well-being of relationships. This mindset maintains care for one's own needs yet enables recognition others will develop differently according to their nature and upbringing.

With positivity, rigid demands dissolve as acceptance replaces resignation. Understood, the context of behaviors shifts from perceived flaws toward opportunities for empathy and mutual understanding. Patience emerges where frustration once festered beneath unrealistic burdens.

Openness to human fallibility nurtures compassion where injury arose from past mismatches. Through this lens, connections cultivate resilience during life's inevitabilities instead of crumbling under their weight. Individuality flourishes alongside care for communal health.

Over time, this recalibrated perspective transforms perceptions from judgment of discrepancies towards celebration of progress however imperfect. Bonds strengthen in their ability to weather variance through patience, forgiveness and belief in continued learning for all parties.

Shifting Your Mindset

Cultivating a framework of positive expectations begins inward through openness to growth. Rigid perspectives rooted over time require conscious effort to reframe receptively. The first step involves establishing honest dialogue to prevent assumptions from inflicting more harm than clarity could heal.

In these discussions, focus on collaboration over accusation by sharing hopes respectfully while emphasizing care, not demands, for others' innate needs and journeys. Make room for diverse realities to coexist congruently versus conformingly through patience.

From there, actively look for virtue where skepticism once lingered. Shift attention toward strengths and acts of care instead of fixating on perceived failures to align perfectly against preconceived rubrics. In doing so, perception transforms problems into possibilities.

Take the example of perceiving a sibling's dependence on parents not as a negative taxing their resources, but as a dynamic upholding familial bonds through mutual uplift. See beyond surface reflections to recognize hidden facets enriching all involved, such as joy in nurturing offspring or preventing loneliness from isolating elder generations.

Open perspective reveals relationships as complex ecosystems, not pass-fail report cards subject to narrow metrics alone. Interdependence and diversity resiliently strengthen the whole where independence and uniformity risk fracture.

Over time, consciously seeking light cultivates tenderness where criticism hardened hearts. Focus shifts from what others lack toward celebrating abundance already shared. Relationships thereby blossom as gardens nurtured by optimism, not weeded for imperfections against idealizations.

With dedicated reframing through compassionate talks and active appreciation, positive expectations bloom where toxic ones withered bonds. Connections naturally deepen through embracing humanity as an interactive spectrum, not pass-fail rubrics demanding impossible perfection.

The Power of Flexibility

One of the benefits of positive expectations is the flexibility it brings. When you're not clinging to narrow, specific outcomes, you're better able to adapt and roll with the flow of life and your relationships.

If you approached every interaction with an open, positive mindset, you'd be less likely to feel thwarted, irritated, or resentful when things don't go exactly as you'd hoped. Instead, you'd be able to appreciate the positive aspects of the experience due to having adjusted your expectations accordingly.

Cultivating a mindset of positive expectations can be a game-changer in your relationships and overall well-being. By letting go of narrow, high expectations and embracing flexibility and positivity, you'll find yourself feeling less stressed, more understanding, and better able to navigate the complexities of human interaction. So, the next time you catch yourself harboring rigid expectations, take a deep breath and consciously shift your mindset.

Focus on the positive aspects of the person or situation, and remind yourself that flexibility and open-mindedness are the keys to a happier, more fulfilling life.

Understand Your Personal Rights

While legal protections govern civic affairs, personal rights concern the intimate relationships shaping our well-being on deeper levels. Beyond statutes, we each hold innate beliefs about dignified treatment befitting our individual humanity. Thus empowering self-awareness arises by discerning our own personal rights derived from our core values.

Whether honesty, loyalty or independence, the qualities given precedence inform reasonable standards for how close bonds ought respect our nature. For example, sincerity as a sanctuary may instill a right to candid yet caring communication from confidants. Our individual experiences further shape these rights as no two journeys exactly align. For example, trust violated in the past compels us to increase our discretion now especially from people we let into our inner circle. Or observing that forgiveness heal a heavy hearts firsthand may nurture compassion as a right afforded to others and given freely.

Defining personal rights involves introspection to uncover the subconscious fingerprints value systems leave upon relationship needs. Take time reflecting upon why certain behaviors feel just or unjust respectively in bonds most intimate. Look also to understand how others may view similar issues variably according to their life lessons.

With clarity, these rights facilitate our personal boundary setting without demand but through empathy. Asserting personal rights stems from compassion to ourselves, not aggrievement to others. They spring from our conscience, not reaction.

Honoring others' personal rights discovered through self-awareness in turn fosters understanding beyond the surface traits of others. Eventually, bonds take root at these deeper philosophical levels where surface interactions may have once cause friction.

Reciprocity and Self-Reflection

As we've looked at our own values and the expectations they create, it's important to be fair. When deciding what behaviors you'll accept from others, think about what you offer too.

Do you treat people the same way you want to be treated? If honesty is important to you, are you honest with others? If you want second chances, do you give them to other people as well?

It's easy to demand things from relationships without thinking about our own responsibility. But that's not a two-way street. We have to be willing to give what we want to get.

Take time to really think about your behavior. Are your expectations the same for yourself as they are for other people? We all make mistakes sometimes. Do you show understanding when others mess up, just like you'd like understanding for your own flaws?

Thinking hard about fairness makes us better partners in relationships. No one is perfect, so we need to be forgiving. If we want respect, we must show respect too.

Relationships work best with give and take from both sides. By making sure we follow the same standards we set for others, we build trust and care between people. That's the goal - treating each other well through both good and bad.

Subjectivity and Setting Boundaries

Figuring out what really matters to us isn't always easy. Personal rights come from inside each person based on what they believe. But what's most important to you may not be the same for someone else. That's okay - we're all different.

The good thing is, understanding yourself better actually gives you power. When you know your values and what you need, you can make clear rules for how people should treat you. You learn to stand up for yourself when something crosses the line.

Some things we think everybody should get, like respect. But personal rights are personal. It's not about forcing others to feel the same way - it's about knowing yourself.

Taking time to learn your values is important. Think about what principles guide you and where they came from. Then you can figure out what kinds of behaviors you're willing to accept from people. Are honest conversations a must? Is privacy something you can't live without? Only you can answer that.

Don't worry if others don't agree exactly. As long as you understand another person's rights may differ, that's okay. What matters is respecting each other even when views don't match up.

Once you identify your personal rights, you gain the power to set clear boundaries. You can tell people no when something goes too far. And you feel comfortable protecting your well-being and happiness.

Looking inside takes courage. But it results in confidence to be your true self. And that's valuable because strong relationships are built on trust and mutual care.

Overall, exploring personal rights benefits both yourself and those around you. You respect individuality while demanding the same. People understand your limits, just as you understand theirs. Differences make space for closer bonds based on shared humanity over surface similarities alone.

Taking the time for self-reflection is worth it. See who you are, know your worth, and use that to define healthy interactions. With clarity on personal rights comes empowerment living fully as your best self every day.

Maintain Your Boundaries

Sometimes people get stuck thinking they are always the victim. Even when it's their own mistake, they act like others made them do it. This can confuse you and make you question what really happened.

But don't worry, it's possible to avoid getting pulled into their way of thinking. Let's look at how to keep your own point of view clear.

Some folks feel better blaming others instead of accepting responsibility. They twist things to look good and paint people as "bad guys". But this is just their way of avoiding the truth.

It's easy to go along with their story to avoid conflict. But that just teaches them you agree with their made-up version of reality. Then they keep dragging you into new problems that aren't really problems at all.

The best thing is to understand each situation yourself instead of believing everything they say. Look at the facts without letting emotions take over. Stick to what truly happened, not somebody's excuses.

If they complain about you, don't get defensive. Calmly share your perspective in a nice way. Let them think what they want while you stay true to yourself.

Some people may get mad when you don't join in on blaming others. But don't worry - you aren't causing the anger. The goal is keeping a clear mind of your own.

Over time, they may realize twisting things doesn't work on you anymore. But even if not, at least you won't doubt the truth or the people in your life. Just stay focused on fair solutions, not made-up stories.

Boundaries mean standing up for honesty without hurting others. It takes practice, but brings confidence handling tough talks in a balanced way.

Disagreement with Toxicity

It's normal to worry someone may get upset when you don't agree with them. But standing up for yourself calmly is important. Even if they react strongly at first, you're doing the right thing by not playing into unhealthy behavior. Some people constantly blame others or twist things to make themselves seem like a victim. They want to pull you into their stories so they don't feel alone. But getting involved just teaches them it's okay to keep doing it.

The best approach is to politely share the real facts on your side when they complain about something that isn't true. Use a calm, kind voice so you aren't adding fuel to the fire. Stick to only correcting made-up parts - don't argue about feelings.

They may keep being mad no matter what. But as long as you kept your cool, you won't regret sticking up for honesty later. And they might think twice before trying the same tactics to pull you back in next time.

Standing up for yourself is healthy and important. You deserve to feel good without someone else's drama. While disagreeing takes courage, you're really just taking care of yourself in a respectful way. Don't worry so much about fixing their behavior. Focus on your own actions staying truthful and kind. In time, they may realize twisting things doesn't work anymore. But even if not, you'll feel better keeping your head clear of distortions.

The goal is setting boundaries with caring, not conflict.

Disengage Early

Some people want others to join in complaining with them. Or they may accuse you in hopes that you'll argue back and get stuck in their story. But don't take the bait!

If they start spinning tales about being a victim, just say something kind yet brief like "I'm sorry you feel that way" and stop talking about it. This response shows you listened without agreeing with made-up details. Shutting down the drama early on is healthier than feeling dragged in.

Resisting long explanations or defenses of yourself takes practice. But it works better than voicing those things, which just gives their claims more air time. A gentle, empathetic reply acknowledges their feelings in a respectful way. But you aren't validating crazy claims or letting nonsense drag on. It's a polite way to end the subject.

They may keep pushing afterward to argue. But stay calm and stand your ground that you won't engage further. Keep answers short if you must reply at all.

With time, hopefully they'll realize twisting events with you goes nowhere. But either way, you're taking care of yourself by avoiding useless back-and-forth drama.

Maintain Your Boundaries

Standing up for yourself is just the beginning. To really keep healthy limits when dealing with toxic behavior, you need to stay strong inside. Remember that other people's feelings or made-up stories aren't your problem to solve. You are in charge of taking care of yourself and setting rules others must respect.

When someone tries to make you feel guilty into believing what isn't true, remind yourself their view isn't reality. You get to choose how to respond. Saying no doesn't mean not caring - it means caring about your own well-being first. Dealing with toxic relationships can be tricky. But if you avoid playing into twisted thinking, you'll feel empowered making your own choices. Don't take on the job of fixing someone else - focus on you.

Your role is protecting yourself, sharing how limits work, and not getting sucked back into drama. This is a learning process of self-care.

With time and practice, staying true to you gets easier. Others may keep at it, but inside you'll know your worth without needing their approval. Freedom comes from trusting yourself over distorted thinking from another.

Remember - putting up with nonsense doesn't help anyone in the long run. Have courage staying calm yet strong.

Believe that handling tricky things with patience and respect for all will help relationships but stay strong on rules of care for yourself first. Know that you have what it takes keeping balance through challenges. You were made for so much more than cleaning up excuses. Stay true to your heart and keep learning daily. With head held high, walk on toward peace through understanding your value without limits from others.

The Manipulator

Toxic individuals and manipulators often go hand in hand. Their behaviors feed off one another and can sneak up on you before you even realize what's happening. It's natural for us to not want to see the worst in those close to us, like friends and family, so we miss the signs of manipulation. But understanding how manipulation works is the first step to protecting yourself from its harms.

What exactly is manipulation? The dictionary definition is "the act of controlling someone or something to your own advantage, often unfairly or dishonestly." At its core, manipulation involves controlling another person's emotions, perceptions, behaviors, or relationships to benefit oneself. Now this doesn't mean every relationship has a manipulator - most human interactions involve some level of influence. However, manipulation crosses a line when it damages trust or takes away another's autonomy for selfish gain.

A common example is how most of us say "I'm fine" when asked how we're doing, even if we aren't really fine. While this seems harmless, it is a form of manipulation because we are controlling how others perceive us. Instead of seeing sadness, anger or depression, they only see that we are "okay." But this mild manipulation is usually unconscious and meant to avoid burdening others with our problems, not to gain something. As long as it doesn't hurt us or others, there's no need to feel guilt.

More troubling forms of manipulation include lying, withholding information, threatening or implying threats, isolating people from their support systems, gaslighting where one denies reality and causes the victim to doubt themselves, using sex coercively, creating an imbalance of power in the relationship, springing negative surprises to catch someone off guard, giving the silent treatment as punishment, and playing the victim role.

The motives behind manipulation vary - it can be conscious or subconscious. Conscious manipulators deliberately use lies, threats or other tactics to control and often harm others for personal benefit. Subconscious manipulators may not realize the damage caused by behaviors stemming from own unresolved issues, like low self-esteem or a need to feel in control. Regardless of intent, the effects on victims can be exhausting physically and mentally as they try to preempt or soothe the manipulator's moods. Over time, this takes a toll on mental wellbeing and the ability to trust others.

Some manipulators have diagnosable conditions like narcissistic personality disorder or antisocial personality disorder where manipulation is a core symptom. But mental illness is not required - manipulative behaviors can also arise from fear, anxiety or a need to control one's environment. The bottom line is that manipulation violates healthy boundaries and the autonomy of others. So how can one protect themselves?

The first defense is awareness - learning to spot manipulative behaviors and their effects. Pay attention to how you feel in certain interactions and relationships. Do you often question your own perceptions or feelings? Do you find yourself regularly making unreasonable sacrifices or compromising boundaries? These can be signs it's time to take a step back and reassess the situation.

Setting clear boundaries is also important. Don't be afraid to say "no" when requests make you uncomfortable. You control your own time, money and wellbeing - don't let anyone make you doubt that or take it away. If possible, discuss concerns with trusted friends or a counselor to gain an outside perspective. Their support can boost confidence to make needed changes.

Finally, remember your inherent worth has nothing to do with any one relationship or person's opinion. You deserve to feel respected and cared for without conditions. If current relationships lack this, it may be time to establish some distance or set new expectations. Prioritizing healthy interactions will preserve both mental wellbeing and the ability to form secure bonds in the future. With awareness and self-respect, no one can manipulate you without your active consent.

Why Is Manipulation So Toxic

While manipulation seems inherently harmful, we don't always recognize its more subtle forms. Advertising is a prime example - companies use psychological tactics every day to influence our purchasing decisions. Think of a product you regularly buy, like laundry detergent or toothpaste. Did careful marketing sow seeds of desire that ultimately changed your brand loyalty?

On surface, this type of influence appears minor, but manipulation works the same in interpersonal relationships. Given distorted or incomplete information, someone can alter our judgments against our interests or well-being. Over time, these subtle infringements on autonomy can seriously damage trust and take a mental toll. So how do we identify manipulation's effects and protect ourselves from toxic situations?

Consider Emily and Jordan's story. For over a year, their relationship seemed loving and balanced. But gradually, Jordan's behavior became controlling without either noticing at first. If Emily wanted a girls' night out, Jordan would insist he had special plans for them instead. Not wanting to disappoint, Emily agreed to cancel her other commitments each time.

As months passed, this dynamic escalated. Jordan discouraged Emily from regular activities like visiting friends or family, working late shifts, or exercising alone. Isolated, Emily lost confidence as Jordan tightened his grip. Her concerned network noticed weight loss and nervousness but Emily brushed off worries, still believing Jordan's affection to be caring rather than possessive.

Had she paid closer attention to subtle changes, Emily may have recognized Jordan slowly cutting social ties that gave her independence. By removing alternative support systems, manipulators can more easily damage self-worth until their target relies solely on their approval for happiness. But how could well-meaning friends have helped Emily see this toxic progression sooner?

The ability to notice manipulation often lies in reflecting on how we feel in relationships. Do we brush off internal doubts and constantly question our own perceptions or needs? Research shows that eroding autonomy through control of activities, information and personal decisions slowly damages mental wellbeing over time.

Had Emily expressed growing discomfort to allies, they could have helped validate her instincts instead of judgments. An outside view may have highlighted dynamics like pressure to abandon plans or isolated her from confidantes as manipulation. Even well-intentioned partners can cross lines through behaviors like gaslighting, threatening consequences for honesty, or exploiting dependency on their affection for decisions.

Awareness, clear boundaries and social support offer defenses. Now, Emily might recognize subtle pressures and feel empowered to say 'no' with backing from those who respect her choice. Building self-worth separate from any relationship provides strength against manipulation by withholding approval as a coercive tool.

What Do Manipulators Have in Common?

Understanding the subtle yet damaging nature of manipulation is an important step towards healthy self-awareness and stronger relationships. While manipulators come in many forms, certain tendencies and tactics frequently overlap. By examining common behaviors and their effects, we can more easily identify concerning relationships and protect our mental wellbeing. Though manipulation often goes unseen due to skillful deception, awareness builds resistance to such toxicity.

Covert Control Through Influence Rather Than Open Requests

Manipulators avoid directly asking others for help or fulfillment of needs, choosing instead to covertly influence their targets through subtle psychological tactics. A healthy relationship involves open communication - if someone required assistance, they would express it respectfully without demanding compliance. Manipulators lack this capacity due to their compulsion to maintain constant control over situations and people. Rather than risk refusal of a direct request, they employ deceptive strategies to maneuver victims into unknowingly providing what is wanted. This infringes on the target's autonomy and ability to make truly informed choices.

Sowing Doubt Through Distorted Narratives

Gaslighting causes its victims to question objective reality and their own perceptions or memories due to the manipulator's skilled denial and distortion of facts. Experts in this technique sow seeds of uncertainty in others through misleading statements, contradictions, and even subtle behaviors intended to induce self-doubt. For example, claiming a request was never made after it clearly was. Or poking at a target's confidence with insinuating remarks like "Are you sure about that?" The cumulative effect erodes mental stability over time as gaslighting chips away at the firm ground of personal experience someone normally stands on. Its covert and insidious nature renders this a profoundly damaging manipulation method.

Redirecting Blame

Projection occurs when people attribute their own negative qualities, thoughts, or emotions to others as a defense mechanism. Manipulators weaponize it by accusing targets of the very traits they themselves possess in order to deflect responsibility and control narratives. This could involve an angry manipulator labeling their victim as perpetually angry regardless of reality. Or a dishonest individual starting to irrationally suspect their partner of identical wrongdoings stemming from their own guilty conscience. Through projection, manipulators stir conflict and chaos while painting themselves as reasonable and their targets as problematic or unstable. It obscures reality and undermines the victim's self-assurance.

Overlooking Nuance With Broad Generalizations

Manipulators minimize taking the time to understand nuanced perspectives by painting others or situations with broad, reductive generalizations. For example, if a stressed coworker vents work issues, a manipulator might tell colleagues said person is "always in a bad mood." This dismisses context to portray the target negatively while sparing the manipulator from addressing root concerns. Generalizations also lack empathy, creating distance to exploit. They damage relationships and promote discord by oversimplifying people into caricatures the manipulator can then define and control through distorted narratives told to others.

Hidden Aggression Under Thinly Veiled "Humor"

Behind the guise of "just joking," manipulators weaponize humor to covertly bully and emotionally harm targets they victimized. Their "jokes" regularly target vulnerabilities or push boundaries to upset the target while gaslighting them into believing their discomfort stems from hypersensitivity. Manipulative jokes are never lighthearted - the intent lies in causing pain through plausible deniability. Targets experience consistent anxiety wondering when the next "innocent jab" will land, leaving emotional bruises that manifest over prolonged exposure to such toxic behavior. By trivializing targets' valid hurt feelings, manipulators further erode self-esteem and isolate them.

Instigating Rifts To Weaken Unity

Sowing division and discord among natural allies is a classic manipulative tactic. This involves portraying selective kindness to some while secretly disparaging them to others, stirring doubts and preventing united fronts from forming against the manipulator's harmful influence. They thrive off generating interpersonal conflict for control. Dividing a core support system through insincere flattery, lies, and exaggerations of what "people are saying" leaves targets exposed and distrusting of potential sources of help. United fronts pose threats, so manipulators prevent them through deliberate relational sabotage for their own gain.

Dodging Responsibility By Shifting Discussions

When conversations approaching a manipulator's accountability commence, their deflection instincts immediately kick in through subject changing. Contrasting healthy discussions where open-minded people address issues directly, manipulators veer discussions onto tangents, new topics, hypotheticals - anything to pivot focus away from unpacking their own actions, emotions or responsibility. By distracting targets from pressing problematic behaviors, manipulators dodge ownership while manufacturing a veneer of cooperativeness they lack. Staying on topic threatens exposure, so it becomes their manipulative debate adversary.

They Use An Elusive Carrot To Ensure Dependence

No matter how much a victim caters to a manipulator's ever-changing whims, the goalposts for their favor or approval will constantly shift further out of reach through no fault but the manipulative design. Manipulators need targets to be kept in a state of chronic self-doubt, chasing an approval that can never materialize no matter what. This breedscodependency, exhaustion, and an erosion of self-worth in victims trying to meet bottomless needs that were artificially manufactured to begin with. True happiness cannot exist where manipulation has bred an environment of perpetual dissatisfaction by dangling the proverbial carrot just out of grasp.

Recognizing manipulation's warning signs empowers our ability to set clear personal boundaries and avoid needlessly compromising oneself for another's selfish motives. With knowledge comes self-determination, free of coercive tactics intended to undermine personal agency and stability.

The Dark Psychology of Manipulation

Understanding manipulation requires examining its foundations in human nature and behavior. Dark psychology delves into these complex topics through an objective scientific lens. At its core, dark psychology aims to understand how and why certain individuals are prone to controlling or influencing others using covert means like deception, especially when it damages trust or autonomy. Insights from this field provide a more well-rounded perspective on toxic relationships and their impacts.

A formative concept in dark psychology is known as the Dark Triad - three antisocial personality profiles linked to manipulation. Researchers defined this triad as narcissism, psychopathy, and Machiavellianism based on their shared traits of selfishness, emotional coldness, and willingness to manipulate others dishonestly for personal gain.

Narcissists exhibit an inflated ego and lack of empathy, seeing others as objects to serve their needs.

Psychopaths can appear superficially charming but act without conscience or remorse for harm caused.

And *Machiavellians* are unscrupulous social climbers focused only on strategic manipulation to dominate any situation.

On surface, the Dark Triad may conjure notions of severe criminals. However, everyday life provides opportunities for even relatively high-functioning individuals to leverage some combination of these traits on a smaller scale through subtle influencing tactics. Simple examples could include stroking someone's ego to extract favors, twisting facts to dodge responsibility, or withholding intimacy as a control tactic in relationships. While milder variants of dark traits alone do not necessarily indicate a toxic person, their amplification and systematic use indicates a tendency toward emotional harm and infringing on others' autonomy.

Covert manipulation often operates through manipulation of emotions. Love bombing someone with gifts and flattery before asking a favor is a tactic to trigger feelings of obligation. Conversely, abruptly withdrawing warmth and attention applies passive pressure. Restricting choices presents an illusion of free will while limiting real options. And reverse psychology invites rebellion by forbidding something, knowing it will arouse desire. Lies and twisted semantics breed uncertainty, another factor that impairs clear decision making.

While manipulation may achieve short term goals, it does so by corroding trust over time. Victims feel mentally and emotionally drained managing manipulators' mercurial moods at their own expense. Isolation from natural support systems leaves them prone to gaslighting and second guessing. This dynamic fosters codependency and stunted personal growth as self-worth becomes entangled with another's fickle approval. Even very subtle manipulations wear away at well-being if constantly endured.

Regrettably, some societies normalize and even encourage using dark psychology. Unscrupulous sales teams may train employees to view customers merely as targets to outmaneuver rather than partners to genuinely help. Dating coaches market manipulation as the key to romantic success. While influence itself is a natural part of socializing, such perspectives cross ethical lines by prioritizing results over respecting others' consent and welfare. A relationship rooted in manipulation cannot foster true care, communication or fulfillment for either party in the long run.

Recognizing Manipulation

Have you ever felt unsure about a situation or relationship due to subtle behaviors that didn't seem quite right? Questioning your own perceptions is a sign manipulation may be at play. The first step is honestly reflecting on key questions without excuses to gain clarity.

Ask yourself simply "yes" or "no" to the following: Is the responsibility truly mine to take on? Will I feel good doing this once any sense of obligation lifts? Am I afraid to say no or worried about potential emotional backlash? Are there clear strings attached that don't sit right? Would this person do the same for me if roles reversed? Does my gut strongly agree or disagree?

Do not feel obligated to anything making you uncomfortable. We all have the right to make our own choices without fear of repercussions. If deep down a request doesn't align with your values or priorities, it's important to trust that voice.

Having open discussions and solid boundaries helps avoid getting maneuvered into situations against your will. Being direct in stating intentions, needs and goals to relevant people makes distortion of facts harder. Documentation of all important communications also creates accountability if behaviors turn questionable later on.

Expanding your inner circle with trustworthy individuals provides additional perspectives to validate how interactions make you feel. With more allies, manipulators find isolating targets more difficult too. Make time to build this support network before potential issues arise.

Should prevention fail, confronting manipulation factually demonstrates your awareness without anger or emotion. Call out concerning actions respectfully while focusing on how they impact you rather than attacking the person. Reactions may be unpleasant, but a manipulator losing control is not your problem to manage. Keep your wellbeing the priority throughout.

With self-awareness comes empowerment over one's choices. Trusting instincts and speaking up for oneself reminds manipulators they cannot override another's free will. While avoiding toxicity altogether remains ideal, recognizing red flags means never feeling trapped by problematic situations or people against our consent. Ultimately, choosing ourselves wisely is the greatest protection against covert influence attempts.

The Sociopath

Let's talk about something that's not exactly a fun topic, but it's crucial to understand: dealing with sociopaths in our lives.

While television and movies often use the terms interchangeably, there is an important difference between a sociopath and a psychopath. Both have antisocial personality disorder, but their exact tendencies and behaviors differ in meaningful ways. Understanding these distinctions can help us navigate relationships with toxic people and choose the best strategies for each situation.

At their core, sociopaths and psychopaths struggle to form genuine emotional attachments with others. Their brains seem wired differently when it comes to understanding and sharing feelings. However, sociopaths and psychopaths exhibit this in distinct manners.

A sociopath has clear disregard for how their actions impact others. Forming caring bonds does not come naturally to them. Work and home life can be challenging because sociopaths struggle to control impulsive behaviors, especially when angry or upset. That said, on some level sociopaths recognize their problematic conduct. They just usually find ways to rationalize or justify hurtful choices after the fact.

Psychopaths have a more deceptive nature. Unlike sociopaths who frankly do not care, psychopaths are capable of feigning compassion. However, this emotional display is merely an act - psychopaths cannot truly connect or empathize. Relationships lack meaningfulness and sincerity for them. While psychopaths may experience attraction or possessiveness, their version of "love" is often cold, empty, and self-serving. It is difficult for partners of psychopaths, as underlying criminal plans or misdeeds may be intentionally hidden beneath a facade of normalcy.

It is critical to note that both sociopathy and psychopathy occur on spectrums. Not all sociopaths or psychopaths engage in the most harmful extremes we see depicted in media. For some, antisocial tendencies are more mild. Psychopaths in particular may desire love and acceptance, even if their behavior sabotages such connections due to an inability to understand others' inner worlds. Violence is a possibility with both, but self-harm can be just as likely an outcome of their disorders.

The differences matter because recognizing sociopathic versus psychopathic attributes informs how best to respond. With a sociopath, their transparency about lack of concern allows clear boundaries - do not expect caring or change abusive conduct. Confrontation may be needed. Psychopaths require strategy since manipulation is easy for them. Do not believe superficial affection or promises at face value without observable alteration. Remain vigilant and prioritize self-protection over hoping a psychopath can reform overnight.

It is also crucial to note that, without diagnoses, toxic people may not understand their own conditions. Many blend sociopathic and psychopathic qualities in unpredictable mixes. Therefore, pay close attention to behaviors, not labels. Focus on your own safety and well-being above all else when navigating relationships impacted by personality disorders.

The Workings of a Sociopath

When trying to understand difficult people in our lives, it can be tempting to leap to conclusions or apply labels we see in movies and media. However, accurately diagnosing complex conditions like sociopathy requires nuanced evaluation from mental health professionals. We must be careful not to assume the worst in others or inflate minor annoyances into catastrophic personality disorders.

One dictionary defines a sociopath as someone unable or unwilling to behave acceptably to society. But what qualifies as "acceptable" changes constantly depending on cultural norms and values. A more precise description is that sociopaths lack empathy - they cannot comprehend or care about how their actions impact others' rights and feelings.

Manipulation often comes naturally to sociopaths. They seem incapable of guilt or remorse over the harm they cause. For example, if someone bangs their head and is in pain, a sociopath won't understand that experience internally. If a sociopath pushed the head, they wouldn't feel regret. This disconnect from others' experiences is a key sociopathic trait.

However, it's all too easy to overdiagnose based on limited observations from our personal lives. With a simple online search, we can start imagining sociopathic explanations for normal relationship conflicts and disappointments. I call this the "Doctor Google Syndrome" - believing we've uncovered someone's true diagnosis because one or two behaviors align with cursory research. But the full clinical picture is far more nuanced.

Remember, we all have moments where our perspectives become detached from others'. Major life stressors like divorce can leave us numb or force us to compartmentalize emotions for survival. Views on controversial topics like gun rights might provoke responses that seem insensitive at a glance but really stem from our own ideological standpoints. Such instances do not prove sociopathy on their own.

Normal human coping mechanisms and individual opinions should not too hastily be labeled pathological. Unless we possess specialized mental health training, it's presumptuous to diagnose friends or family. Even therapists need extensive evaluation periods and diagnostic criteria confirmation before arriving at conclusions involving severe personality disorders with criminal implications.

When relationships sour, our instinct is to assign blame and paint the other person as the villain. Yet the truth is usually far more complex, with layers of understandable human flaws on both sides. Instead of reactionary labeling, try approaching others and yourself with empathy, understanding we all struggle at times to bridge our differences. Focus on open communication to resolve specific issues versus making damaging characterizations that can damage trust and intimacy long-term.

Still, if you notice some of these typical characteristics and behaviors in your relationships, it is best to take the safest and most effective actions so that you can start living your life freely.

Here are some of the signs that could help you to identify a sociopath:

A total absence of empathy: Imagine talking to someone about your worst day ever, and they respond with all the emotion of a brick wall. That's what interacting with a sociopath can feel like. They might say the right words, but there's no real feeling behind them. It's like they're reading from a script titled "How to Act Like You Care." They can't put themselves in your shoes because, frankly, they don't want to. Your feelings? Not even on their radar.

Acting on impulse without a second thought: You know that little voice in your head that says, "Maybe this isn't such a great idea"? Sociopaths don't have that. They're like a kid in a candy store, grabbing at whatever catches their eye without considering the consequences. Only instead of a sugar high, their impulsive actions often lead to chaos for those around them. They might quit a job on a whim, blow all their money on a crazy scheme, or jump into and out of relationships faster than you can say "red flag."

Using scary tactics to pull the strings: A sociopath's go-to move? Turning up the fear factor to get what they want. They're not above making threats or getting aggressive to keep people in line. It's like they're always playing a twisted game of "Simon Says," where Simon is a bully and the stakes are way too high. They might threaten to spill your secrets, harm themselves, or even get physical. It's all about keeping you off balance and under their thumb.

Charm and smarts as weapons of manipulation: Here's where sociopaths can really throw you for a loop. They can be incredibly charming and intelligent, using these traits like a spider uses its web. They'll dazzle you with their wit, make you feel special with their attention, all while slowly wrapping you up in their manipulative schemes. It's like being hypnotized by a really charismatic snake - fascinating, but dangerous.

Lies, lies, and more lies: Truth is a foreign concept to a sociopath. They'll spin tales faster than a novelist on deadline, all to get what they want. And the scary part? They're often really good at it. They lie about big things, small things, and everything in between. It's like they have an allergy to honesty, and the only cure is personal gain.

Never learning from past mistakes: You know how they say, "Fool me once, shame on you; fool me twice, shame on me"? Well, a sociopath will keep trying to fool you, and everyone else, over and over again. It's like they're stuck in a time loop where consequences don't exist. They'll make the same mistakes, hurt the same people, and never seem to learn anything from it.

Struggling to build real connections: For a sociopath, relationships are like disposable cameras - use them once and throw them away. They might have a lot of acquaintances, but deep, meaningful relationships? Those are as rare as a unicorn sighting. They just can't (or won't) invest the emotional energy needed to form real bonds with others.

A rap sheet that keeps growing: Some sociopaths take their disregard for others to the extreme, racking up a list of crimes that would make a career criminal proud. From petty theft to violent outbursts, they see laws as mere suggestions. It's like they're playing Grand Theft Auto, but in real life, and without the reset button.

Responsibility? What's that?: Ask a sociopath to take care of something important, and you might as well be asking them to fly to the moon. They dodge responsibility like it's a game of dodgeball, and they're the champions. Work, bills, commitments - these are all things that happen to other people, not them.

Substance abuse as a way of life: Many sociopaths turn to drugs or alcohol, not as a social lubricant, but as a full-time lifestyle choice. It's like they're trying to fill the empathy-shaped hole in their personality with substances. Of course, this only tends to amplify their other problematic behaviors, creating a vicious cycle that's hard to break.

If you've got someone in your life who's ticking all these sociopathic boxes we just talked about, it's time to put on your emotional armor. Think of it like this: you wouldn't stick your hand in a lion's cage and expect not to get bitten, right? Well, the same goes for keeping a sociopath close - it's a recipe for getting hurt. Your mission, should you choose to accept it (and trust me, you should), is to build some serious boundaries. I'm talking Fort Knox-level protection for your emotional well-being. And let's be real for a second - you're not Captain Save-a-Sociopath. Trying to fix them is like trying to bail out the Titanic with a teaspoon - it's not gonna happen, and you'll probably go down with the ship. Instead, focus on surrounding yourself with people who are more like emotional trampolines - they bounce you higher, not drag you down into the mud.

How to Spot a Sociopath

Those toxic people in your life, the ones who always seem to leave you feeling drained or manipulated, might not be running around like villains in a superhero movie, but that doesn't mean they're not causing real harm. Here's the thing: sociopaths and psychopaths (folks with antisocial personality disorders, or ASPD for short) are like master illusionists. They're not all out there committing crimes that make the evening news. Nope, they're often walking among us, blending in like chameleons. They're experts at hiding the behaviors they don't want you to see, kind of like how a magician never reveals their tricks.

Now, you might be thinking, "Surely I don't know anyone like that!" But here's a reality check that might make you sit up straighter: studies show that about 1% of people have psychopathic traits. That means if you know 100 people, odds are you've crossed paths with one. And sociopaths? They're even more common. We're talking about 4% of the population, or one in every 26 people you know. That's not just a drop in the bucket - it's more like a whole glass of water!

So, how do you spot these folks before they start pulling your strings? Well, we've already talked about some red flags, but let's dive a bit deeper. Let's look at some real-world examples of how people with ASPD might behave.

#1. They know how to work their charm

Let's talk about charm - that special something that makes some people irresistible. Most of us know someone who can light up a room just by walking in. But here's the thing: there's a big difference between natural charm and the kind used by folks with antisocial personality disorders (ASPD).

Think about your most charismatic friend. Their charm is probably pretty consistent, right? Whether they're chatting with the boss or the new intern, they're just naturally pleasant to be around. It's like a warm, steady glow. But people with ASPD? They're like social chameleons. Their charm isn't steady - it's adjustable. They can crank it up or down depending on who they're talking to. It's like they have a built-in radar that tells them exactly what each person wants to hear.

Picture this: An ASPD person at a party. They spot a shy introvert in the corner and dial their charm way down. They approach quietly, speak softly, creating a bubble of intimate conversation. The introvert feels understood, maybe for the first time that night.

Then they see the life of the party - a bubbly extrovert. Watch as they crank that charm up to eleven. Suddenly, they're cracking jokes, laughing loudly, matching the extrovert's energy perfectly. Before you know it, they're the center of attention. It's like they're playing a video game, and charm is their superpower. They can adjust it on the fly for each new "character" they meet. And they're really good at it.

Now, being able to communicate well with different types of people isn't bad in itself. But for people with ASPD, it's not about genuine connection. It's about control. They use this chameleon-like charm to manipulate situations to their advantage.

So, what's the takeaway? It's not about becoming suspicious of every charming person you meet. But it is about trusting your gut. If someone's charm feels too perfect, too tailored to your exact preferences, it might be worth taking a step back and asking yourself why.

#2. They try to influence your opinion of others

It's normal to meet someone new, like them at first, and then change your mind if you notice things about them that don't sit well with you. That's just part of getting to know people. But when someone with antisocial personality disorder (ASPD) is involved, things can get a bit messy.

Here's what it might look like: You meet a new coworker and think they're pretty cool. Maybe you grab lunch together a few times and enjoy chatting. But then, out of nowhere, another coworker (the one with ASPD) starts whispering in your ear. "Did you hear what they said about you in the meeting?" or "You know they're just using you to get ahead, right?"

At first, you might brush it off. But they keep at it, dropping little hints and comments that make you doubt your new friend. It's like they're planting seeds of doubt in your mind, and before you know it, those seeds have grown into full-blown mistrust.

This is a classic move for someone with ASPD. They're not just sharing office gossip - they're actively trying to shape your opinions and control your relationships. It's like they're the puppet master, and they want to be the one pulling all the strings.

Why do they do this? Well, it could be for a few reasons. Maybe they feel threatened by your new friendship. Or perhaps they just get a kick out of manipulating people's feelings. Whatever the reason, it's not cool.

So, how can you spot this behavior? Pay attention to how often someone talks about others behind their backs. If they're constantly trying to make you think badly of other people, that's a red flag. Trust your own judgement about people, and don't let others make up your mind for you.

Remember, healthy relationships are built on trust and respect, not gossip and manipulation. If someone's always trying to turn you against others, it might be time to take a step back and ask yourself why they're so interested in controlling who you like or don't like.

#3. They behave inconsistently

Now, we all have moments where we change our minds about people. Maybe you had a misunderstanding with someone, talked it out, and became friends. That's normal and healthy. But when we're talking about folks with antisocial personality disorder (ASPD), it's a whole different ball game.

These people can flip-flop their loyalties like they're changing TV channels. One minute they're whispering in your ear about how awful Sally from accounting is, and the next they're having lunch with Sally and laughing like they're old pals. It's not just confusing - it can feel like a real betrayal.

So why do they do this? Well, it all comes down to a lack of real emotional connections. For most of us, friendships are built on trust, shared experiences, and genuine care for each other. But for someone with ASPD, other people are more like game pieces on a board. They'll move them around however it suits them best at the moment.

Think of it like this: Imagine you're playing a video game where you can be friends or enemies with different characters. You might choose to be friends with one character because they help you complete a mission. But once that mission is over, you might switch to being their enemy if it helps you level up faster. That's kind of how people with ASPD see relationships - it's all about what they can gain.

This behavior can show up in all sorts of ways. Maybe they're the office gossip, always stirring up drama between coworkers. Or perhaps they're the friend who's always pitting people against each other, enjoying the chaos they create. They might even be the family member who plays favorites, constantly switching who they support in arguments.

The tricky part is, they can be really good at explaining away their behavior. "Oh, I just misunderstood the situation before," they might say. Or, "I'm just trying to see both sides." They always have an excuse ready, and it can make you doubt your own perceptions.

So, how can you spot this kind of disloyalty? Pay attention to patterns. Does this person often bad-mouth others behind their backs? Do they frequently change their opinion about people depending on who they're talking to? Are they always in the middle of some kind of drama or conflict?

True friendship isn't about always agreeing or never having conflicts. It's about being there for each other, respecting boundaries, and treating each other with kindness and honesty. Anyone who can't offer that consistently might not be someone you want in your inner circle.

#4. Blame Shifting

Picture this: You're trying to have a calm chat with your friend about something that's bothering you. Maybe they forgot your birthday or bailed on plans last minute. You're just looking for a simple "I'm sorry, it won't happen again." But instead, suddenly you're the bad guy!

They might say things like, "Why are you always so dramatic?" or "I can never do anything right in your eyes!" Before you know it, you're the one apologizing, even though you didn't do anything wrong. It's like they've waved a magic wand and *poof* - they're the victim, and you're the villain.

This isn't just annoying - it's a classic manipulation tactic. People with ASPD are often experts at turning the tables. They don't want to take responsibility for their actions, so they make you feel guilty instead. It's like they're holding up an emotional mirror, reflecting all your concerns back at you.

And it doesn't stop there. They might use this same trick to explain why they don't get along with others. "Oh, Sarah from work? She's always out to get me," they might say. Or, "My ex was crazy - that's why we broke up." Notice how it's never their fault? The tricky part is, they can be really convincing. You might start to doubt yourself. "Am I being too sensitive?" you might wonder. "Maybe I am overreacting."

So how do you deal with this? First, trust your gut. If something feels off, it probably is. Second, stick to the facts. If they try to derail the conversation, gently bring it back to the original issue. And remember, it's okay to set boundaries. You don't have to play their game.

#5. The Rules don't apply to them

Sociopaths ahve this weird idea that rules are for everyone else, but not for them. It's like they think they've got a "Get Out of Jail Free" card for life. Sound familiar? This is pretty common in folks with antisocial personality disorder (ASPD).

Here's the thing: these people aren't dumb. Far from it. They're often smart cookies who totally get the rules. Whether it's the rules of a board game, social norms, or even laws, they understand them just fine. But understanding and following are two different things in their book.

Imagine playing Monopoly with someone who keeps "forgetting" to pay rent when they land on your property, or who somehow always has an extra $500 in their pile. That's kind of how these folks operate in real life. They know the rules, but they just don't think they apply to them.

This attitude shows up in all sorts of ways. Maybe it's the coworker who always takes credit for other people's work. Or the friend who consistently "forgets" to pay you back. Or even the family member who thinks it's okay to borrow your stuff without asking.

It gets really obvious when money's involved. They might think nothing of fudging their taxes, or "borrowing" from the company coffers. In their mind, they're special, so why shouldn't they get special treatment?

The tricky part is, they often have a way of justifying their actions. "I work harder than everyone else, so I deserve this," they might say. Or, "It's not a big deal, everyone does it." They've got an excuse for everything.

#6. They get you to share secrets

Now, having a good friend to confide in is great. But when we're dealing with someone who has antisocial personality disorder (ASPD), things can get tricky.

Here's how it might play out: This person starts showing a lot of interest in you. They're always there to lend an ear, asking questions about your life, your feelings, your worries. It feels nice, right? Like you've found someone who really gets you.

But here's the catch - they're not doing this because they genuinely care. For them, it's like they're gathering information for later use. Every secret you share, every fear you admit to, every insecurity you reveal - it's all filed away in their mental folder labeled "Things I Can Use to Manipulate This Person."

Think of it like this: Imagine you're playing a video game, and you're telling another player all your character's weaknesses. In a friendly game, that's fine. But what if that player is actually your opponent? Suddenly, all that info becomes a weapon they can use against you.

That's kind of what's happening here. They're collecting your emotional "weak spots" so they can push those buttons later when they want something from you.

Now, you might be wondering, "How can I tell if someone's genuinely interested or if they're just collecting info?" Well, here's a clue: People with ASPD generally aren't that interested in others' emotions. So if someone who usually doesn't care much about feelings is suddenly super keen to hear all about yours, that's a red flag.

Also, pay attention to how they use the information you share. Do they bring up your insecurities when they want something from you? Do they use your fears to make you feel guilty or scared? That's not what a real friend does.

#7. They change their stories

Someone with antisocial personality disorder (ASPD) might tell you one story about their weekend, then tell your friend a completely different version. Why? Because they're always changing their stories to fit what they think each person wants to hear or to get something they want.

The problem is, after a while, they've told so many different versions that even they can't keep track of what they've said to who. It's like they're juggling a bunch of different stories, and sooner or later, they're bound to drop one.

Now, you might think, "Aha! I've caught them in a lie!" But here's where it gets really tricky. When you point out that their stories don't match up, they don't admit they lied. Nope, they flip it around on you.

They might say things like, "You must have misheard me," or "Why are you always trying to catch me out?" Suddenly, you're the one feeling confused and doubting yourself. You might even start to wonder if you're being paranoid.

This is all part of their game. They're really good at making you question your own memory and judgment. It's like they're trying to rewrite reality, with them as the author and you as a character who doesn't know what's real anymore.

#8. Show no remorse

For people with antisocial personality disorder (ASPD) It's like they're missing the part of their brain that says, "Oops, I messed up. I should feel bad about that."

Here's what it looks like: Let's say someone with ASPD borrows your favorite shirt without asking and spills coffee all over it. A typical person would feel terrible, apologize, and offer to replace it. But someone with ASPD? They might just shrug it off like it's no big deal. They might even act like you're overreacting for being upset.

It's not that they don't understand they did something wrong. They get it, alright. They just don't care. It's like they're watching a movie of their life instead of living it - they see the mistake, but they don't feel any emotional connection to it.

This lack of remorse shows up in big and small ways. They might lie to your face and not bat an eye. Or they could hurt someone's feelings and not see why they should apologize. It's like they're playing a game where other people's feelings don't count.

The tricky part is, sometimes they might say sorry if they think it'll get them something they want. But it's not a real apology - it's just words to them, not a genuine feeling of remorse.

Dealing with a Sociopath

Your safety should always be the top priority if interacting with a sociopathic individual, especially one with a history of violence. If you feel threatened in any way, do not hesitate to get help immediately.

It can be difficult to seek outside involvement with someone you care about. But please do not downplay warning signs or tell yourself their behavior was just a one-time thing if they have acted aggressively. What may start as an isolated outburst could escalate and escalate over time. You do not want to find out too late that this person has attacked before, and you feel responsible for not speaking up sooner. Their violence could also potentially harm others one day if not addressed.

Have a discreet escape plan ready just in case. Prepare a "go bag" with important documents, spare cash, an extra phone, and a copy of your car keys stored somewhere accessible if needed fast. You may also want a separate bank account in your name alone, even with a small balance, to help get to safety. This advance planning will give you options if a hazardous situation arises unexpectedly.

If staying with friends or family is not an option, do not hesitate to contact local domestic violence shelters. Their services can help you through this difficult time, particularly if children are involved whose wellbeing must be prioritized as well. When devising strategies, focus on quick, stealthy exits whenever the sociopath is not home to reduce risks.

Of course, leaving should only be considered as an absolute last resort in truly dangerous scenarios. Most interactions may remain non-physical. However, constant vigilance is important when sociopathy is a known factor, even without outward threats, as empathy deficits could put others at emotional risk. Maintain healthy boundaries and do not believe excuses that downplay unacceptable conduct. Learn to recognize subtle manipulation tactics early.

Here are some techniques that will help you deal with and protect yourself from sociopaths:

1. Don't try to fix them

Attempting to change a sociopath is rarely successful and may make the situation worse. Sociopaths often are not aware of or willing to acknowledge their own behaviors and deficiencies in empathy. Qualified mental health professionals provide the only effective treatment through long-term therapy. As caring as one's intentions are, an individual lacks the training to effectively help a sociopath overcome antisocial personality disorder. Focusing change efforts on oneself is healthier than hoping to alter another.

2. Protect your privacy

Sociopaths are skilled manipulators who will use any details about someone for their own gain without regard for how it impacts the other person. Sharing too much personal data, like salary, relationships, or private work matters, arms a sociopath with ammunition for control and abuse. The less they know about one's vulnerabilities, the less power they wield to hurt or take advantage. Protecting privacy self-preserves dignity and limits opportunities for manipulation.

3. Trust your instincts

When constantly second-guessed by a sociopath's distortions, it's normal for self-doubt to creep in. But our instincts evolved for survival and still offer guidance. Pausing interactions to check inwardly provides clarity. If something feels off, there's usually a reasons even if past mistakes cloud perception. Have confidence that inner warning signs indicate manipulation is at play rather than reacting rashly in the moment. Staying grounded in one's authentic experience, not a sociopath's fabricated reality, fosters healthy decision-making.

4. Be firm on your boundaries

Well-defined, unwavering boundaries form the cornerstone of protecting one's well-being around sociopaths. What behaviors one finds acceptable or not must be clearly communicated and held through insistence when pressured. Example limits like living together but not co-mingling finances allow autonomy within relationships. Firmly saying no, even to beloved people, shields from compromise done solely to appease at one's own cost. Personal boundaries maintain safety.

5. Find a compromise

While some lines can never be crossed, other issues allow flexibility that respects both parties' stances. Compromising in good faith where room exists averts power struggles dangerous for the empathetic person. As one example, maintaining separate accounts alongside a joint one for shared costs balances individual control with cooperation. Dialogue seeking understanding from each side can locate middle ground. But one should never compromise principles or safety.

6. Walk away when necessary

Anger serves no good purpose and is what sociopaths desire to see. Leaving heated interactions instead of escalating displays mature self-control and takes their power away. Distance allows processing emotions healthily rather than reacting rashly. When calm, the situation frequently looks different enough to address constructively. If not, separation reinforces boundaries. Making space prevents feeding sociopathic need to provoke and maintains dignity through self-regulation.

7. Spend time with others

Nourishing relationships with caring peopleboosts well-being and inner strength challenging to build alone. Others demonstrate healthy bonds are possible, provide perspective sociopaths distort, and offer unconditional support navigating complex dynamics. Filling life with nurturing connections outside toxic ones dilutes sociopaths' capacity to impact life satisfaction and self-worth. Community adds fortitude for difficult decisions empowering the individual.

8. Actions speak louder than words

Promising change rings hollow without behavioral evidence, as words are easy but change requires long-term effort. Focus on patterned actions, not superficial speeches, which alone indicate whether someone grew or aims to manipulate further. As the saying goes, fool me once with falsehoods but ongoing deceit reflects only on oneself. Reformation must be observable, not just heard, particularly for those whose disorder means using lies for control habitually without guilt. Seeing, not hearing, is believing.

9. Talk to a professional

While sociopathy negatively impacts others, its toll also weighs heavily on those subject to manipulation daily. Counseling provides skilled assistance making sense of complex dynamics and associated distress. A counselor brings objectivity when darkness clouds perspective through no fault of one's own. Their expertise helps devise strategies maintaining mental wellness in stressful interpersonal contexts. Not enduring alone preserves health and hope through understanding with an compassionate ear. Outside help lightens a heavy load.

10. Know when it is best to end the relationship

As painful as departing intimacy may feel, one's well-being takes priority over all else. When manipulation, violation of boundaries or personal safety become too severe despite attempts at resolution, terminating the connection becomes necessary self-care, not a shortcoming. But safely exiting means total no-contact cessation; no half-measures allow further disruption. Blocking all avenues of interaction with the sociopath protects from further harm or hoovering attempts at re-establishing power and control. One's peace follows letting go.

Healing After a Sociopathic Relationship

Ending a relationship with a sociopath is an ordeal that takes immense courage and inner strength. These individuals are skilled at manipulation, deception, and control techniques that leave victims questioning reality and depleted emotionally. While removing oneself from the toxicity is the healthiest choice, it initiates a challenging journey of recovery and rebuilding.

The trauma bonds formed through intermittent reinforcement and confusion tactics can seem near impossible to sever. Strong urges to reconnect or seek validation tempt at vulnerable moments. Self-doubt creeps in as the sociopath likely paints their ex in an unflattering light to sway mutual contacts. Isolation intensifies due to not wanting others to perceive one as "crazy." These hurdles seem insurmountable alone.

However, with support, effective coping strategies, and commitment to self-care, survivors can regain empowerment and flourish free from the sociopath's influence. The process requires patience as wounds deepened over time cannot fully mend overnight. But each small victory—resisting a hoovering attempt, facing a trigger without faltering, or making healthy choices in moments of weakness—strengthens resolve.

Here are some tips and tricks to help you move past this type of toxic relationship:

Maintaining No Contact – Resisting the urge to reach out is critical but challenging. In weak moments, we rationalize a quick message won't hurt. However, any contact risks the sociopath manipulating back in. Their behavior patterned on control means even innocent exchanges reopen old emotional wounds. By blocking all avenues of communication totally, space opens to heal freely without their interference. While concern for others comes naturally, focus caring on supportive network instead of the sociopath draining energy. Time and distance strengthen resolve against future manipulation.

Leaning on a Support System – Isolation encourages rumination, so turn toward empathetic listeners. Close confidants understand one's experience from a caring place rather than judgment. When missing the sociopath or relationship seems overwhelming, discuss reasons for leaving to regain clarity. Reminders center on self-protection instead of dwelling in darkness alone. Sharing burdens lightens them while distancing from toxic influences trying to hoover one back. Community anchors hope that better relationships exist where feelings are mutual.

Identifying Triggers – Acknowledging triggers like holidays and milestones that stir emotions prepares to face them constructively. Rather than suppressing uncomfortable feelings, express them through writing, art or talking it out to release mentally. Have soothing rituals prepared involving soothing activities, comforting food or time with understanding company. Trigger-related stress inevitably fades over time as new joyful memories develop untainted. Each time a trigger loses power to disrupt progress confirms resilience and independence.

Self-Care is Paramount – To fully detach takes effort and patience. Focusing on healthy activities boosting well-being like yoga, cooking nourishing meals or nature walks replaces empty thoughts. Getting sufficient rest and practicing relaxation strengthen resilience to resist hoovering attempts. Growth happens gradually through extended self-focus - be gentle judging improvements in the mirror rather than against perfection. Each small victory over codependency cultivates empowerment as control shifts entirely inward toward nourishment.

Embracing a Growth Mindset – Reframing "starting over" as a blank canvas avoids connotations of failure or loss associated with past mistakes. Freedom exists to design life authentically without manipulation dampening passion. Rather than judging oneself for not immediately "bouncing back," see adversity as an opportunity to reinvent with wisdom gained. Every challenge makes space to actualize dreams unconstrained before due to sociopathic influence. Each lesson hard-won cultivates skills spotting red flags sooner to avoid future harm.

Finalizing No Contact – Resolving for good means deleting or archiving any reminders in photos or messages perpetuating rumination. Close all points of social media interaction definitively without lingering looks "checking in." If items strongly connected to the relationship cannot yet be purged, pack them away out of sight until ready to release control fully. While severing ties feels like mourning a loss initially, it opens room for healthy partnerships where care is mutual and consistent. With time and patience, new adventures replace past pain.

The road to full post-traumatic growth after a sociopathic relationship is long, yet each step forward signifies growing distance from past harm inflicted. As triggers fade and manipulation attempts no longer disrupt progress, survivors stand empowered with insight and resilience against future vulnerabilities. While scars may remain, they symbolize endurance of battles ultimately overcome rather than lifelong wounds.

Looking back, it is easy to see how far autonomy and well-being have blossomed since severing toxic bonds. New routines prioritizing fulfillment have replaced whatever portions of identity were chipped away through gaslighting and control. Surrounding with healthy support shows real care looks nothing like what was confuse for love in darkness before. Hope for thriving partnerships founded on empathy, communication and equality grows each day further removed from psychological abuse.

For those still in active struggle, know that light does find its way through even the deepest night. Asking for help from counselors or programs meant to lift burdens carried too long validates rather than weakens resilience. Temporary pain inevitably gives way to recovery, so hold fast to vision of a calm future where triggering memories disturb peace far less than before. Each small choice nudging closer to that destination matters greatly.

The Narcissist

Dealing with difficult people can take a real toll on our mental and emotional well-being. One type of toxic person that many struggle with is the narcissist. Their selfish behavior and lack of empathy causes pain for those in relationships with them. While I don't pretend to be an expert on psychology, having witnessed the struggles of loved ones opened my eyes to this topic. In this chapter, I hope to provide some context around narcissism and tactics for handling narcissists in your life.

First, it's important to truly understand what narcissism is. Nowadays, people throw around labels like "narcissist" as insults without knowing the clinical definition. This waters down the meaning and minimizes those with real Narcissistic Personality Disorder (NPD). According to psychology experts, narcissism stems from the Greek myth of Narcissus who fell in love with his own reflection. At its core, narcissism is an inflated sense of self-importance and entitlement. People with NPD expect to be seen as superior and special. They require constant admiration to feed their fragile ego.

Some key traits of narcissists include a lack of empathy, demanding perfection from themselves and others, and extreme envy or rage when they don't get what they want. Though they may seem confident, deep down narcissists have very low self-esteem that they try to hide. Any criticism is seen as a threat rather than an opportunity for growth. Due to lacking empathy, narcissists can't understand how their selfish actions affect people. They also believe they should be catered to at all times and not receive blame for anything. If their unrealistic expectations aren't met, anger and depressive episodes may result.

Those close with narcissists know how draining it is to constantly have your worth and accomplishments undermined. Their moods are also very unpredictable. One day they put you on a pedestal, and the next you don't meet their needs so they tear you down. Such manipulation and lack of stability does a real number on your mental health over time. Additionally, narcissists rarely think they are wrong. So getting them to acknowledge hurtful behavior or consider other perspectives is nearly impossible without professional help.

Given these challenges, it's best to be aware of narcissistic traits before committing deeply to a relationship with someone displaying them. The reality is narcissists rarely change without committing to long-term individual therapy. So ultimately, you need to decide if salvaging the relationship is worth ongoing distress or if it's time to remove this negative influence from your life for good. Prioritize your mental wellbeing and surround yourself with people who respect you as an equal human being. With these tactics and surrounding support, you can learn to reclaim your power away from manipulative and selfish behavior.

Distinguishing Self-Confidence from Narcissism

It's common for people to admire traits like self-assurance and confidence. However, there is an important distinction between healthy self-confidence and narcissism. The former represents a balanced and secure sense of self, while the latter involves an inflated ego and need for constant validation. Knowing the difference can help us avoid toxic relationships and behaviors.

True self-confidence stems from believing in one's capabilities without undermining others. Confident individuals set reasonable goals and tackle challenges by acknowledging both strengths and weaknesses. They recognize achievements but do not feel the need to constantly boast or one-up people. Most importantly, confident people feel comfortable celebrating successes of friends and partners without jealousy.

Relationships based on confidence are built on mutual respect and trust rather than surface value transactions. These individuals prioritize listening to understand others' perspectives in conversations. They also own mistakes and learn from experiences rather than blaming externally to protect fragile egos. Constructive criticism is received as helpful feedback rather than a threat.

Confident people's self-worth does not depend on praise from external sources. They engage in regular self-reflection to improve upon areas for growth. While proud of accomplishments, there is awareness that no one is perfect. Importantly, humble confident people make space for others to shine too without insecurity.

On the other hand, narcissism involves an inflated and unrealistic sense of importance. These individuals expect special treatment and constant admiration due to entitlement. Narcissistic traits include lack of empathy where only their opinions seem valid without concern for how actions impact others.

Relationships are centered around what the narcissist gains rather than equal partnership. Constructive criticism is not tolerated, often resulting in angry outbursts or blame-shifting. But beneath the confident exterior lies deep insecurity requiring constant validation.

Narcissists avoid genuine self-reflection that could challenge their inflated self-image. Success is measured by status and one-upping competitors rather than personal fulfillment. While they may feign interest in others' wins, envy often lurks below the surface. Vibrant relationships are replaced with facade interactions that serve the ego. Here are some key signs:

Empathy: The Heart of the Matter

Have you ever poured your heart out to someone, only to feel like they weren't really listening? That's what it's like talking to a narcissist. They're about as empathetic as a brick wall. Sure, they might nod and make the right noises, but their mind is already racing ahead to how they can turn the conversation back to their favorite subject - themselves.

Now, confident folks? They're a whole different story. They're the ones who can put themselves in your shoes, offer a shoulder to cry on, and give you their undivided attention when you need it most. It's like they have this superpower of really getting where you're coming from.

I remember chatting with a friend who'd just been through a tough breakup. She told me how her confident buddy sat with her for hours, just listening and offering support. No judgment, no rushed advice - just pure empathy. That's the kind of friend we all need, right?

Relationships: It Takes Two to Tango

Let's talk about relationships. A confident person sees relationships as a two-way street. They're all about give and take, mutual respect, and building something meaningful together. It's like a beautiful dance where both partners get to shine.

But for a narcissist? Relationships are more like a one-man show, and guess who's the star? That's right - they are. They view every interaction as a chance to boost their ego, gain something for themselves, or show off how amazing they are. It's exhausting, really. Being in a relationship with a narcissist is like being a prop in someone else's life story.

I once knew a guy who seemed super confident at first. But as time went on, it became clear that every conversation, every decision, every plan had to revolve around him. His girlfriend felt more like an accessory than a partner. That's not confidence - that's narcissism in action.

Handling Mistakes: To Err is Human

We all mess up sometimes, right? It's part of being human. A confident person gets that. They can hold up their hand and say, "Yep, I goofed. My bad." They see mistakes as learning opportunities, not personal failings.

Narcissists, though? They'd rather eat a cactus than admit they're wrong. They'll twist themselves into knots trying to explain why it wasn't really their fault, or why their mistake was actually a stroke of genius that you're just too dumb to understand. It's like watching a contortionist at a circus - impressive in a way, but ultimately kind of sad.

I once worked with a guy who never admitted to making a mistake. Every error was someone else's fault, every missed deadline was due to "unforeseen circumstances." It created a toxic environment where no one felt safe to take risks or be creative. On the flip side, my current boss is quick to own up to her mistakes and it's created a culture where we all feel comfortable learning and growing together.

Self-Reflection: Mirror, Mirror on the Wall

Self-reflection is another area where the difference really shows. Confident people are like scientists of their own lives. They're curious about themselves, always looking for ways to grow and improve. They welcome feedback - even when it's a bit uncomfortable - because they know it can help them become better versions of themselves.

Narcissists? They avoid self-reflection like it's a contagious disease. Looking inward might mean confronting some uncomfortable truths, and that's just not their style. They've built this perfect image of themselves, and they'll do anything to protect it - even if it means living in a fantasy world of their own creation.

I had a coworker who would bristle at any suggestion for improvement. Constructive criticism? Forget about it. She'd either ignore it completely or find a way to turn it back on the person giving the feedback. It was like watching someone build a fortress around themselves, brick by brick, until they were completely isolated from reality.

Sharing Success: Rising Tides and All That Jazz

Lastly, let's talk about how they handle success - both their own and others'. Confident people are like cheerleaders for life. They celebrate their own wins with joy and gratitude, but they're just as excited when good things happen to others. They know that someone else's success doesn't diminish their own.

Narcissists, however, treat success like it's a limited resource. They hoard their own achievements, showing them off at every opportunity. But when someone else succeeds? Watch out for the green-eyed monster! They might pretend to be happy for others, but inside, they're seething with jealousy or looking for ways to take credit for someone else's hard work.

I once attended a team celebration where a project had been a huge success. While most of us were congratulating each other and sharing the credit, one team member kept steering the conversation back to his contributions, downplaying everyone else's role. It was uncomfortable, to say the least, and really dampened the celebratory mood.

Understanding these differences can make a huge difference in your personal and professional life. It can help you build healthier relationships, set better boundaries, and even improve your own self-confidence, without crossing the line into Narcissism.

Remember, true confidence isn't about being perfect or never making mistakes. It's about knowing your worth, valuing others, and always striving to grow.

Improving Self-Awareness

It's not enough to simply observe narcissistic behaviors in others. We must also reflect regularly on our own actions and interactions. Doing so can provide valuable insight into strengthening relationships through healthier behaviors.

Ask yourself important questions like: Do I make an effort to understand other perspectives through active listening and empathy? Or am I primarily focused on having my own views validated? How do I perceive my close bonds - are they built on mutual care and respect, or do I see relationships more transactionally in terms of what others can offer me?

Can I admit flaws and mistakes without feeling deeply flawed as a person? Being imperfect is human, but a willingness to improve is what separates maturity from fragile ego. Am I open to constructive feedback to better myself, or do I dismiss criticism out of fear it may threaten my self-image?

When people I care about succeed, am I genuinely happy for their accomplishments? Or do feelings of envy sometimes emerge that I try masking with fake praise? Answers to queries like these indicate where we fall on the spectrum between confidence and narcissism.

It's crucial to note that occasional moments of vanity or seeking reassurance don't inherently signify clinical narcissistic personality disorder (NPD). Consistent behaviors across all areas of life that severely impact one's well-being and relationships with NPD suggest seeking professional help.

If reflecting highlights traits like inability to empathize, defensive reactions to feedback, or unstable relationships due to selfish behaviors, talking with trusted companions could provide a different perspective. Close ones may notice habits we are blind to see.

Mentors, counselors and mental health experts also offer guidance tailored for specific circumstances. Their support can help target unhealthy patterns through tried techniques before issues intensify. But the first step begins from within - developing self-awareness.

With practice, we gain clarity on where to strengthen compassion towards others. Approaching life's challenges and people around us with humility, gratitude and care ultimately leads to relationships founded on mutual understanding and growth. Toxic tendencies holding us back can be transformed through dedicated reflection and openness to change.

By distinguishing confidence from narcissism, we pave the way for connections built to empower both parties. This knowledge moves us closer to liberation from self-absorption through balanced self-worth respecting humanity in all people. Our interpersonal well-being and community are strengthened as a result.

The Different Types of Narcissists

Let's dive into the wild and wacky world of narcissism, shall we? Just like there's more than one way to skin a cat (not that we're advocating for that, mind you), there's more than one flavor of narcissist out there. It's like a twisted ice cream shop where every scoop leaves a bad taste in your mouth.

The Healthy Narcissist: A little narcissism is normal for everyone. Recognizing personal strengths while still respecting others is healthy. Occasional pride in achievements doesn't meet the criteria for NPD.

The Overt Narcissist: This extraverted type craves attention and feels superior. They lack empathy and disregard boundaries to stay the center of focus. Attention-seeking and arrogance are prominent traits.

The Covert Narcissist: More introverted than overt narcissists, covert types also desire praise but cannot handle criticism. They are sensitive yet envy others' success. Issues are exaggerated while dismissing people's genuine problems.

The Malignant Narcissist: Taking narcissism to a disturbing degree, malignant types enjoy inflicting pain on others through manipulation. Highly intelligent yet sadistic, they are difficult to deal with due to masking harm with clever tricks.

The Psychopathic Narcissist: Rare but dangerous, psychopathic narcissists feel no remorse and can become violent. Their aggression may escalate to criminal behaviors like serial killing due to lack of empathy.

The Somatic Narcissist: Obsessed with physical appearance and fitness, somatic narcissists prioritize their own needs above all else for their image. They demand others acknowledge their looks or physique.

The Cerebral Narcissist: Touting intelligence as proof of superiority, cerebral narcissists belittle others to make themselves feel bigger. No debate or discussion satisfies their constant need to assert mental dominance.

The Bullying Narcissist: Taking narcissism into the realm of persistent aggression, these types socially mock and degrade people to meet internal insecurities rather than external goals. Cruelty becomes a personality trait.

The Sexual Narcissist: Focusing narcissism onto sexuality, sexual narcissists manipulate through seduction and rarely remain faithful. They view partners as objects to bolster their self-perceived performance prowess.

The Love Bombing Narcissist: Showing unusually over-the-top affection upfront, love bombers draw people into committed relationships before revealing narcissistic abuses. The technique masks true intentions for control through faux intimacy.

The Celebrity Narcissist: Gaining noteriety and fame, some acquire narcissistic tendencies inflated by constant public praise. Without grounding, wealth and status can warp one's self-perception as more significant than reality.

Identifying the Narcissist in Your Life

Now that we've covered definitions and types of narcissists, you should have a better idea if you're involved with one. Let's examine further telling signs to look out for:

- Initial interactions were amazing but quickly soured over time. Narcissists "love bomb" to draw people in before showing their true colors.

- They dominate conversations by controlling topics and speaking far more than others. Narcissists need constant attention on themselves.

- They fish for compliments to boost low self-esteem through praise from others.

- Your emotions, needs, and feelings are rarely acknowledged or cared about by the narcissist due to lacking empathy.

- Few to no long-term fulfilling friendships exist, as narcissists view people as disposable once their usage expires.

- Gaslighting occurs, making you question your own sanity through persistent denial and lies meant to confuse.

- Apologies are nonexistent along with compromise, as narcissists cannot admit fault or see outside perspectives.

- Leaving the relationship provokes panic, rage and smear campaigns when supply sources diminish.

- Overly controlling behaviors establish power and supply constant attention to inflate ego.

- Personal responsibility is dodged through blame shifting or excuse making to preserve image.

- Everything is seen in extremes of good or bad with little nuance or understanding of gray areas.

- Projecting negativity deflects their own shortcomings onto others through harsh criticism.

- They struggle forming cohesive team work due to transactional views of relationships and poor listening skills.

It's important not to imagine issues that simply don't exist. Everyone has imperfect moments at times. For example, forgetting a single bill is a minor oversight, not a narcissistic tendency. Look for signs that repeatedly emerge across interactions rather than overanalyzing isolated incidents.

We all exhibit some narcissistic traits now and then which is considered normal and even healthy in moderation. But several of the behaviors regularly appearing may suggest a deeper issue, warranting further reflection. Don't obsess over labels either, as what matters most is how you feel in the relationship and if needs are being met. Trust your gut instincts and prioritize well-being above all else.

What Can You Do If There Is a Narcissist in Your Life?

Dealing with narcissistic people is tough when avoiding them isn't possible. Maybe it's a family member or coworker. In these situations, boundaries are key. Why? Because narcissists don't care how their actions make you feel. They'll ignore complaints. Boundaries avoid arguments by stating clear rules upfront.

Boundaries come from within- Think of an imaginary bubble around yourself. Reflect on recurring problems. What exactly crosses a line for you? For example, public criticism may be okay with close friends but not strangers. Or you feel no criticism in front of others is okay. Only you know your boundaries.

Narcissists will break rules anyway, so have consequences ready – Continuing the criticism scenario from before - you may leave each next time it happens. Give a simple warning: "Don't insult me publicly or I'm gone without talking." State your boundaries, then end talks to avoid manipulation. Narcissists want control. Boundaries give it back by not discussing things.

Have confidence following through on consequences – Focus on consistency, not reaction. Over time, this trains healthier behavior and breaks old harmful patterns. Nobody is perfect. Reflect on how interactions really made you feel, not small mistakes. Look for repeated issues hurting you instead of one-offs.

Care for yourself first – If the same problems continue despite efforts, removing yourself fully may be best. You deserve relationships built on care, trust and respect. Boundaries make dealing with unavoidable narcissistic folks easier. Set clear rules for how you accept being treated. Have consequences to prove limits matter.

Don't engage in their games – Dealing with narcissists means not falling for their mind games. Now you know their tactics and can see manipulation coming. But reacting only gives them ammunition. The best response is removing that power. When they say something to get a rise out of you, simply respond "Okay" and move on. Don't give them something to twist back at you.

Choose battles wisely – If it's a small thing, "Okay" suffices. But if they cross a line, stand up for yourself calmly without anger or blame. You have every right to call out harmful actions respectfully. Do not accept feeling bad because of someone else. You can admit mistakes and care about others. But do not doubt yourself due to another's projections. You alone control your emotions and actions.

Lower expectations – It's natural to hope someone will understand your perspective one day. But realistically, that likely won't happen. Stop waiting for empathy or a meaningful chat to materialize. Focus on moving forward.

Leave the past in the past – You now understand how to handle this person. Bringing up old situations changes nothing and keeps interactions negative. Stay present-minded instead of dwelling.

If upset gets too much, reach out for help – Talking to caring people lightens burdens. A therapist provides solace too. You don't need to struggle alone - others want to support your well-being. Prioritizing your mental health prevents damage from ongoing toxicity. You deserve fulfilling relationships and peace of mind.

With time and experience, interacting with narcissists becomes easier through boundaries and refusing to internalize mistreatment. Stay strong yet calm. Your happiness relies on self-care, not others' validation or approval.

Ending a Narcissitic Relationship

Ending any relationship can be difficult, regardless of gender. Even when a narcissist didn't truly love you, your real feelings for them remain. It's natural to cling to hope things might change, despite current circumstances.

This applies whether the relationship is romantic or not. While parents can't be replaced, finding compassionate people to love and be loved by provides fulfillment instead.

The first step to getting free is ensuring you're fully ready. "Break up-make up" patterns commonly occur, going back and forth on decisions without resolution. This only prolongs pain with a narcissist since they won't alter behaviors. Being certain avoids returning to toxicity.

Next, consider practical details. If a partner, plan living arrangements. Are friends shared where limited contact may happen? Could family gatherings involve seeing each other? For toxic coworkers, figure out complete removal if possible.

When able, a clean break produces the cleanest slate. If some contact cannot be avoided, strict boundaries must minimize further harm. Limit sharing private information or relying on them emotionally/financially too.

Grieving the loss takes time. Allowing sadness shows self-compassion rather than fighting emotions. Processing lets light return after darkness passes. Support from compassionate listeners eases suffering.

Focus daily on self-care activities bringing joy instead of dwelling on past wrongs. Spend time with people boosting your mood rather than tearing you down. Self-love through hobbies and goals redirects energy from what was into new beginnings.

Healing happens gradually. Be patient yet persistent putting your needs first to fully recover strength. An inner secure sense of self persists regardless what others think or say about you.

With distance, perspectives clarify over wounds. While some impacts linger, lessons learned prevent similar unhealthy situations going forward. Each new day rewards by living fully for yourself again at last. Better days are ahead when refusing to accept less than true care and respect.

Plan what you'll say when ending the relationship. Preparing brings confidence without needing long speeches. Let them know it's no longer healthy and you're moving forward alone. Defend your choice if needed, but don't justify endlessly. Give yourself time to grieve. Sadness shows self-care rather than suppression. Don't expect instant happiness - healing takes consistent work. Refer to supportive people and goals on hard days to avoid lingering in sadness alone.

With freedom, reconnect positive connections lost. If parents caused pain, perhaps past romance rekindles. Contact kind souls from life chapters forgotten. Build a network uplifting your journey as strength returns through their caring presence.

Writing negative traits provided perspective. Pour truths out until mind emptied onto paper. Collecting evidence eased moving past toxic impacts. Throw mementos and list away, closing that chapter for good.

Notice life's beauty despite darkness. Though positivity feels foreign after constant negativity, keep an eye open each day. Look beyond what once was done and see what is, whether sunny skies or tiny joys. Therapy also guides perspective shifts for those struggling most.

Endings allow for new beginnings. Stay determined yet compassionate within yourself throughout this process as you deserve relationships where care, trust and respect.

Avoiding Narcissists

After toxic relationships, it's natural to unintentionally seek similar dynamics due to familiarity. Give yourself time alone before committing again to truly discover yourself. Review what happened, learn from mistakes, understand your needs. Slowly release stored trauma from your body through mindfulness. Intuition protects by hearing inner warnings.

In future relationships with others, avoid prejudging based on past hurts alone. New people deserve fair chances too. If old patterns emerge though, remove yourself promptly to prevent repeated pain. You deserve healthy interactions.

Start fresh but listen closely to sensations signaling danger. Leaving toxic ties means protecting yourself from recurring harm. Your well-being matters most but many personalities toxify lives undeserving of mistreatment. Future discussions address additional damaging people preventing joy and growth.

Stay diligent yet kind within. Hard work freed you from oppression; maintaining boundaries keeps it that way. Dark times form through negligence; brightness comes from compassion for yourself as a worthy soul deserving to shine. While wary, remain open-minded. Judge based on present conduct, not past wrongly defining new acquaintances. Your worth goes untouched by others' poor actions or opinions. Walk proudly.

Healing takes patience. Faith in your value liberates from unhealthy holds. Let wisdom guide decisions promoting fulfillment instead of fear. Happier phases await when refusing misery and embracing and kindness for yourself as a person of significance. Brighter days are coming.

The Bully

Bullying is a serious issue that a lot of people struggle with, so I want to help explain what's really going on and how you can start to regain your power in those toxic situations.

Bullying happens when someone repeatedly treats others in cruel or unfair ways to make themselves feel bigger or better. The bullies always pick on people they think are weaker - whether that's because they're younger, smaller, or maybe just seem vulnerable in some way. It isn't just a one-time fight or insult either - bullying is when someone keeps intentionally harming or putting others down over and over.

The bullying can take many forms too. A lot of times it happens through mean name-calling or making fun of how someone looks, acts, or what they like. Sometimes the bullying is even physical, with shoving, hitting, or other aggressive behavior. Other bullies use threats to scare people, spread harmful rumors, exclude others from groups, or now even cyberbully by posting mean things online.

Research shows bullying is most common between the ages of 11-13, when kids are going through a lot of changes and figuring themselves out. Younger kids are more likely to hit, kick, or physically fight, while older kids usually bully through relationships instead - by gossiping, leaving people out, or manipulating friendships. No matter the age though, being bullied can make anyone feel terrible about themselves.

Where does most of this bullying take place? Sadly, a big part happens right at school or on the playground, where bullies often find their targets. Studies show that around 1 in 5 students report being bullied at some point while at school. It affects both boys and girls at similar rates too. And with social media so prevalent, cyberbullies can torment others even away from the classroom.

So why do people bully? There are a few factors that often drive this toxic behavior. Some bullies feel powerful or cool when they put others down, since it makes them feel superior. Others bully because they're going through their own personal problems at home. And peer pressure or wanting to fit in with a certain crowd can also motivate cruel behavior. Regardless of the reasons though, no one deserves to feel afraid or insecure just for being themselves.

The good news is there are strategies for dealing with bullies and taking back your power.

The Root of Bullying

Have you ever wondered what makes a bully tick? It's not as simple as "they're just jerks." There's a whole mess of reasons why someone might turn into a pint-sized tyrant or a full-grown menace. Let's break it down, shall we?

First off, bullying works. At least in the short term, it gets them what they want, like a toddler throwing a tantrum in the grocery store. Sure, it's obnoxious and makes everyone uncomfortable, but if it gets them that candy bar they wanted? Mission accomplished. Bullies use their nasty behavior as a shortcut to get what they want. It's not pretty, but it's effective.

But here's the thing- bullies aren't born wearing leather jackets and demanding lunch money. They're made. And it starts way earlier than you might think. Remember that "terrible twos" phase that makes most parents want to tear their hair out? That's a crucial time for toddlers to learn how to play nice with others. If adults don't consistently put the kibosh on aggressive behavior, kids don't learn to pump the brakes on their own. It's like trying to housetrain a puppy by randomly yelling "No!" every once in a while. It just doesn't work.

A Twisted View of the World

Now, let's take a peek inside the bully's head. It's not a fun place to be. These folks have a whole different operating system running up there. They're not big on being nice to others (shocker, I know), and anxiety? Not really their thing. But the real kicker is how they see the world around them.

Imagine walking around all day thinking everyone's out to get you. That's the bully's reality. They're like those conspiracy theorists who think the government is hiding aliens in Area 51, except instead of little green men, they see hostility everywhere. Someone bumps into them in the hallway? Must be a personal attack. A classmate doesn't share their snack? Obviously a deliberate slight.

And here's the real mind-bender - despite all this paranoia, bullies often think they're hot stuff. It's like they're living in their own personal fan club meeting. Everyone else might think they're a jerk, but in their own minds? They're the coolest thing since sliced bread.

A Lonely Crowd

You might think bullies are swimming in friends, what with all that social dominance they're always flexing. But here's the truth - their relationships are usually about as warm and fuzzy as a cactus. Whether it's with parents or peers, bullies tend to have a hard time connecting.

Think about it - would you want to hang out with someone who's always looking for ways to put you down or use you? It's like trying to cuddle with a porcupine. Sure, you might stick around for a while if you're scared of them, but genuine friendship? Not likely.

It's Not About You

Now, if you've ever been on the receiving end of bullying (and let's face it, who hasn't?), I want you to tattoo this next bit on your brain: It's not about you. I know it feels personal when someone's going out of their way to make your life miserable, but here's the truth - it's all about them.

Remember that messed-up worldview we talked about earlier? That's what's driving the bully's behavior, not anything you've done. You could be the nicest, most inoffensive person on the planet, and a bully might still target you just because you happened to sneeze funny one time.

Understanding this doesn't make the bullying okay - not by a long shot. But it can help you cope. It's like dealing with a yappy dog - knowing that it's barking because it's scared or poorly trained doesn't stop the noise, but it might help you feel less like it's a personal attack on your right to walk down the street.

Why Bullies Pick Their Targets

So if bullying isn't about the victim, why do bullies zero in on certain people? Often, it's because they see their target as a threat. Now, I know what you're thinking - how can that scrawny kid with the thick glasses be a threat to the school's star quarterback? But remember, we're dealing with bully logic here.

In the bully's twisted mind, anyone who's different is a potential threat. Maybe you're smarter than them, or funnier, or people just seem to like you. To a bully, that's like waving a red flag in front of a bull. They feel threatened, so they lash out to try and knock you down a peg.

The thing is, bullies often don't even realize they're feeling threatened. It's all happening in their subconscious, like some kind of messed-up autopilot. They just know they don't like you, and their go-to response is to make your life miserable.

The Bully's Favorite Ride

We live in a world that's obsessed with power. Just look at any superhero movie - it's all about who's the strongest, who can beat up the most bad guys. Some people take this way too seriously and decide that the best way to feel powerful is to make other people feel small.

This is especially common in schools or social circles where there's a clear pecking order. Bullies use aggressive behavior like a shortcut to the top of the social ladder. It's like they're playing a real-life game of "King of the Hill," and they're not afraid to push others down to stay on top.

Sometimes, this power trip is all about instilling fear. Bullies get a kick out of seeing others cower before them. It's like they're starring in their own little horror movie, with everyone else as the terrified victims. And the worst part? They don't care who gets hurt along the way.

The Bully's Twisted Justice

Now, here's a curveball for you - sometimes, bullies think they're the good guys. I know, it sounds crazy, but hear me out. In some cases, bullies genuinely believe their victims wronged them (or someone they care about) in the past. It's like they've appointed themselves judge, jury, and executioner in some twisted kangaroo court.

Of course, whether this belief is based in reality is another story entirely. Maybe the "wrong" was something as minor as looking at them funny one time. But in the bully's mind, it's justification for all sorts of nasty behavior.

Now, let's be crystal clear here - this doesn't make bullying okay. Not even close. If someone's done you wrong, there are proper channels to deal with it. You know, like talking it out, or reporting it to the appropriate authorities. Becoming a bully yourself is like trying to put out a fire with gasoline - it just makes everything worse.

In some really messed up cases, bullies target innocent kids because they themselves were victims of abuse or violence. It's like they're trying to reclaim some of the power that was stolen from them. Again, this doesn't excuse their behavior, but it helps us understand where it might be coming from.

Cyberbullying and Anonymous Attacks

The internet has given us a lot of great things - cat videos, instant access to all human knowledge, the ability to order pizza without talking to another human being. But it's also opened up a whole new arena for bullies to do their dirty work.

Cyberbullying is like the evil twin of regular bullying. It's got all the nastiness of face-to-face bullying, but with the added bonus of anonymity. Some cyberbullies hide behind fake accounts, lobbing insults and threats like a sniper hiding in the digital bushes. It's the ultimate coward's move - all the "fun" of hurting someone, none of the risk of getting punched in the nose.

Not all cyberbullies hide, though. Some are bold enough to use their real names and faces. But even then, there's a distance that emboldens them. It's a lot easier to be cruel when you don't have to look your victim in the eye. And here's the really twisted part - some cyberbullies get a kick out of the attention their nastiness gets. Every like or share on their mean comments is like a little pat on the back, encouraging them to keep up the awful behavior.

When Bullying Turns to Sadism

Now, we're about to wade into some really murky waters. Brace yourselves, folks. Some bullies aren't just acting out of insecurity or a misguided attempt at social climbing. Some of them are straight-up sadists. They enjoy causing pain and misery. It's like they get a twisted thrill out of seeing others suffer.

These are the really dangerous ones. Most bullies have at least a shred of conscience buried deep down. But sadistic bullies? They're operating without that crucial piece of human machinery. They don't feel remorse or guilt. To them, hurting others isn't just a means to an end - it is the end.

This kind of bullying isn't limited to the schoolyard, either. We see it in abusive relationships, in workplaces with toxic bosses, even in criminals who target specific types of victims. It's a dark side of human nature that's hard to face, but we need to be aware of it if we want to protect ourselves and others.

When Victims Become Bullies

Here's a plot twist for you - sometimes, the bully you're dealing with used to be a victim themselves. It's like a messed-up version of "pay it forward," except instead of kindness, they're passing on pain.

These former victims-turned-bullies are often still wrestling with their past trauma. Maybe they were bullied themselves, or suffered abuse at home. Instead of dealing with these issues in a healthy way, they've let them fester and grow like a toxic mold in the basement of their psyche.

Some of these bullies have convinced themselves that bullying others is the only way to stay safe. It's like they're living by some twisted version of "the best defense is a good offense." In their minds, if they're the ones doing the bullying, they can't be victims again.

But here's the thing - this strategy is about as effective as using a chocolate teapot. All it does is perpetuate the cycle of bullying, creating more victims who might go on to become bullies themselves. It's a vicious cycle that keeps spinning, leaving a trail of hurt and damaged psyches in its wake.

So, after all this doom and gloom, where does this leave us? Are we just stuck in an endless loop of bullying and pain? Not necessarily. Understanding why bullies do what they do is the first step in breaking this cycle.

By recognizing the motivations behind bullying, we can start to address the root causes. Maybe it's about teaching better coping skills to kids before they turn into bullies. Or providing better support for victims so they don't turn to bullying as a misguided form of self-protection.

For those of us who've been on the receiving end of bullying, understanding can be a powerful tool for healing. Knowing that the bully's actions say more about them than about us can help ease some of the pain and self-doubt that bullying leaves in its wake.

And for society as a whole? Well, maybe if we can start seeing bullies not as monsters, but as deeply flawed, often hurting individuals, we can find more effective ways to address the problem. It doesn't mean excusing their behavior - far from it. But it might mean finding ways to help them change, rather than just punishing them and perpetuating the cycle.

Factors That Impact Bullying

Research has also shown that there are a variety of factors that can impact why people bully. Some of these include:[2]

- **Sex differences**: While boys and girls are equally likely to be bullies, boys experience more physical bullying, while girls experience more verbal and indirect bullying.

- **Age differences**: Peer bullying tends to decrease as children age, but older kids are also more likely to experience online bullying.

- **Differences**: People who are perceived as different from the majority status group due to physical appearance, disability, race, nationality, color, immigration status, gender expression, or religion are more likely to experience bullying.

The Impact of Bullying

Let's talk numbers for a second. Bullying isn't just some rare occurrence that happens to "other people." It's as common as bad coffee in a cheap diner. Get this: one in three kids - that's right, one-third of our little munchkins - have been bullied in the last month alone. It's like a twisted lottery where the "prize" is misery.

And here's the real kicker: bullying doesn't just hurt the kid being picked on. It's like a stink bomb in a crowded room - everyone gets a whiff. The bystanders? They're not off the hook. Watching this stuff go down can mess them up too. And the bullies themselves? They're not winning any prizes either. It's like they're digging their own emotional graves.

So next time you hear about bullying, remember: it's not just "kids being kids." It's a widespread problem that's leaving a trail of hurt feelings, damaged self-esteem, and messed-up social skills in its wake.

Effects on People Who Are Bullied

Being bullied is never easy to go through, and it can really mess with how a person feels both emotionally and physically. Those having to deal with bullies may struggle with their mental health, like feeling more anxious or depressed over time. Their sleep and appetite can even change as stress takes over.

It's common for kids being bullied to feel very lonely and cut off from others. The mean behavior can make them want to avoid school or activities where the bullying happens. In really bad cases, victims may even think about ending their own life just to escape the constant attacks. That's how deeply hurtful bullying can be to someone's well-being.

People who are targeted might withdraw from friends and stop doing things they used to love and look forward to. Their grades and attendance at school can start to drop too if the bullying is constant and they don't feel safe on campus. Some students really do end up leaving school early because of the toll it takes.

Bullying can also negatively impact careers later in life. Adults experiencing bullying or harassment at work may take more sick days hoping to avoid harsh environments or abusive colleagues. Over time, that kind of toxic stress will damage anyone's health.

If you've been bullied, it's important not to deal with the intense emotions alone. Seeing a counselor or therapist can really help work through tough feelings like low self-esteem, anger, or isolation that bullying often causes. They're trained professionals who can offer coping strategies. Talking to someone you trust can be a relief and first step to feeling better.

Effects on People Who Witness Bullying

It's also important to remember that bullying doesn't just hurt the people being targeted - those who see it happen deal with negative impacts too. Kids witnessing mean behavior between their classmates may develop mental health issues as well over time. Things like feeling more anxious or depressed are common.

In fact, bystanders are at higher risk of using substances like drugs and alcohol to self-medicate those intense emotions. Their attendance at school can start slipping too if the environment feels toxic or stressful. Who wants to stick around somewhere they have to watch their friends be ridiculed and humiliated? It's understandable why witnessing such cruelty would impact someone.

Beyond mental health, onlookers also struggle with emotions like guilt for not stepping in. They may replay scenarios in their head wondering what more they could have done to stop the bullying. It's unfair to expect kids to be heroes, yet the desire to help can lead to a lot of "what ifs." Feelings of shame over not defending victims are tough to work through alone.

In workplaces, when employees have to stand by and observe abusive behavior, it poisons the whole environment. Employees may feel like targets themselves if they get on the bully's bad side. No one wants to spend time in a place filled with such hostility. It's no wonder observers have higher turnover rates - who could blame them for wanting to escape that negativity?

Whether as kids in school or adults on the job, witnessing cruelty toward others should never be minimized. Support should be available for bystanders going through their own pain so they don't think they're alone in how it impacts them either.

Effects on Bullies

It's easy to think bullies don't face consequences for their cruel actions, but research shows they're severely impacted too in both the short and long term. Bullies tend to struggle with substance abuse like alcoholism more often compared to others as they look for ways to cope with whatever personal issues drive their behavior. Their school performance also takes a hit, with higher dropout rates.

Instead of focusing on their future, bullies are more prone to risky decisions at younger ages. Things like getting into physical fights, early sexual activity, and criminal behaviors become more common for them. Once they enter adulthood, these same bullies have trouble maintaining healthy relationships. Rates of spousal or child abuse are higher in those with a history of bullying others.

Work can be just as problematic for bullies who don't change their ways. While some manage to climb career ladders through intimidation, the stressful environments they create take a heavy toll. Employees of bosses with a past of bullying experience seriously low morale, burnout, and heavy turnover. Productivity suffers greatly in toxic workplaces.

No surprise, such conduct opens bullies up to formal complaints, investigations, and even lawsuits related to harassment or unsafe working conditions later. Their choices catch up with them through these consequences. While rehabilitation remains possible, the ripple effects poisons even their own lives in the long run if they don't address contributing personal issues behind the behavior.

So in truth, bullies aren't really winners - bullying is a lose-lose scenario all around for the bully as much as the victim and bystanders involved. The damage circulates widely through communities in different ways.

Stop the Bullying

Bullying is a serious issue that negatively impacts victims, bystanders, and even bullies themselves. While anti-bullying efforts have brought greater awareness, cruel treatment of others still persists in many schools and communities. To truly overcome this problem, a comprehensive approach is needed that addresses the root causes fueling bullying and promotes overall well-being for all. This response will explore two key components of an effective strategy - modifying incentives for toxic behavior, and cultivating cultures of care, empathy and support.

Not rewarding bad behavior

Many people think that as anti-bullying efforts have grown, bullies are less able to get away with their actions. Unfortunately, this isn't always true. Sometimes bullying is unintentionally encouraged even when we don't mean to support it.

For one, bullies can actually gain attention and feel powerful from putting others down. Some kids may bully because they notice other bullies getting what they want through threats and meanness. As long as bullying works to get bullies what they want, the behavior will keep happening.

Ignoring bullying is another way it ends up rewarded. When we see bullying but don't step in to stop it, the bully learns there aren't real consequences. As long as no one intervenes, bullies won't stop on their own. Not taking action rewards them with getting away with hurting others.

Pretending we don't see bullying is just as bad. It leaves victims to deal with problems alone while we look the other way. But if we stand by, how do victims know we have their backs? Silence is just as damaging as the bullying itself.

We also can't assume bullying will never target us or people we care about. Turning a blind eye doesn't stop cruelty - it only empowers bullies to choose their next targets. Our schools and workplaces should be safe spaces for all people.

Fostering mental health and wellness

While understanding why someone might bully is good, prevention is key too. Providing support through counseling, healthy friendships, and anti-bullying programs can help stamp out cruelty before it starts.

These programs benefit not only current victims but also witnesses impacted by bullying they see. We all need care when coping with hard emotions from toxic situations. With compassion, even those who bully might learn better ways of handling what drives them to put others down.

Money, popularity or other advantages won't justify intentionally harming another person. No one deserves that kind of treatment. At the same time, being targeted isn't a reflection of weakness - anyone can become a victim of cruelty through no fault of their own. Role playing how bullying feels is one effective way to build empathy in kids who may bully others or just stand by. Experiencing a situation from someone else's perspective can encourage people to intervene when witnessing unfair treatment of peers.

Promoting wellness for all lays the groundwork needed to transform cultures that bully into ones supporting each individual's inherent worth. With open hearts and understanding on every side, this kinder world becomes possible.

How to Handle a Bully

While bullying often comes to mind as a problem kids face, unfortunately adults can deal with it too in places like the workplace. But just like for kids, there are strategies for regaining control in toxic situations.

First things first - don't internalize a bully's cruel words or actions. Easier said than done when someone's purposely putting you down, but try not to let it shake your self-confidence. Bullies prey on people they perceive as weak or vulnerable. Don't give them the power to make you feel that way.

Staying composed is also important when standing up to an adult bully. Losing your cool won't do any good - stay factual, don't get emotional or accusatory. Clearly tell them their behavior is unacceptable and needs to stop. Then report it right away in writing to HR or a supervisor. Create a paper trail in case it continues.

Some choose to directly confront the bully, but that risks making things worse if they double down. An alternative is complaining to HR with coworkers so you band together in numbers like kids facing down a school bully. It's much harder for an adult bully to retaliate against multiple people all at once. Safety in numbers applies just as much here.

If direct confrontation seems too risky, distancing yourself from the bully is another option. Limit unnecessary solo interactions and communicate primarily through email or messages for documentation. Spend as little one-on-one time with them as possible for your own protection.

Cultivating strong allies and mentor relationships in your workplace helps too. Don't be afraid to open up to others you trust about the distress caused by ongoing bullying or intimidation. Their support can encourage you to keep standing your ground instead of losing hope.

And as a last resort, consider whether the job or relationship remains a mentally and physically safe environment worth staying in. Some organizations or even groups of friends simply won't properly address bullies, so taking care of your well-being may mean finding a new enviornment that values respect. You deserve to feel secure where you spend your time.

With advocacy, a supportive network and healthy strategies to deal with conflict, nobody deserves to tolerate bullying as an adult either. Take care of yourself first - your worth isn't defined by those who try putting you down.

Other Toxic Behavior

What does it mean when we call someone or something "toxic"? This is a term that gets thrown around a lot these days, but have you ever really stopped to think about what it signifies on a deeper level? While we've all had moments where our own behavior has been less than ideal, truly toxic people can take it to an extreme that severely impacts those around them. So in this chapter, I want to delve a bit deeper into understanding just what constitutes toxic behavior and how we can recognize when someone crosses the line from being an imperfect human to a truly toxic presence in our lives.

We have to start by acknowledging that we're all human - that includes both you and me. None of us is perfect, and we've all said or done things at one point or another that have unintentionally hurt someone else. A single toxic incident does not inherently make a person toxic. Where do we draw the line then between someone who occasionally acts out in an unhealthy way versus someone who is consistently toxic? That's an important distinction to make.

For behavior to be considered truly toxic, it needs to chronically cause conflict, distress, or unhappiness for those interacting with that person. In other words, it's a pattern of actions rather than a one-off event. Now, we've all had moments where our words or actions have stressed out a friend or family member before making amends. That occasional outburst alone doesn't brand you as a toxic person. The difference lies in one's ability to recognize when they've crossed a line, take responsibility for their actions, and make sincere efforts to do better going forward. Toxic people, on the other hand, rarely see anything wrong with their behavior and are unlikely to apologize.

So what exactly does consistently toxic behavior look like? For one thing, toxic individuals are often manipulative. You may find their moods and treatment of you to be inconsistent and confusing. One minute they're upbeat and happy, the next they're complaining about how terrible their life is and seemingly looking for attention or sympathy. Being around these types of people tends to leave you feeling uncomfortable or insecure about yourself.

Drama and chaos also seem to follow toxic personalities. If there's no real-life drama occurring, they have no issue creating some of their own. They thrive on the theatricality of conflict and volatility. A major way they stir the pot is by regularly overstepping other people's boundaries - whether it's barging into private conversations or issues, imposing on your personal space or time, or priming inappropriate subjects against your wishes.

To make matters worse, substance abuse can also be a problem with some chronically toxic individuals. Now, enjoying an occasional drink or using recreational drugs does not an toxic person make. But if someone's substance use starts interfering with your life by causing irresponsible or dangerous behavior, it's fair to view it as part of a larger toxicity issue.

Toxicity stems from ingrained patterns rather than a diagnosed mental condition like narcissism or sociopathy. That's not to say the toxic person doesn't have their own unresolved inner demons fueling their actions. But unlike clinical disorders, toxicity is defined more by its detrimental impacts on relationships and daily functioning rather than its origin within the person themselves. With this broader understanding, we can now recognize red flags and better protect ourselves from unnecessary toxicity in our lives. In the next section, we'll unpack some strategies for doing just that.

Identifying a Toxic Person

While toxicity itself is not officially recognized as a clinical diagnosis, it's likely that some underlying psychological condition contributes to toxic behaviors in people. Various disorders have been linked to increased toxicity, such as certain personality types, mood disorders, and trauma-related issues.

Interestingly, many toxic personalities exhibit traits that resemble narcissism, bipolar disorder, borderline personality disorder, and even antisocial behavior. For example, a person with narcissistic tendencies may be more prone to selfish actions that disrespect others and cross boundaries. Meanwhile, someone experiencing bipolar highs and lows could fluctuate wildly between overconfidence and depression in ways that imbalance relationships.

Of course, having any psychological disorder does not predetermined someone to become toxic. But exploring these common psychological roots can give us clues about why certain behaviors may emerge. In this section, our focus is not the causes but rather learning to recognize the red flags of toxicity so we can better protect ourselves from harmful interactions...

Inconsistency

One of the most unsettling qualities of toxic people is their tendency toward inconsistency. As humans, it's natural that we experience ups and downs in our moods and life circumstances from time to time. Toxic individuals, however, take inconsistencies to an unhealthy extreme.

Their behavior fluctuates wildly, making it almost impossible to know where you stand from one moment to the next. They may express excitement about plans with you only to later cancel without reasonable explanation. Toxic types have trouble following through on commitments - whether it's showing up on time, remembering important dates, or fulfilling obligations they previously agreed to. You can never be quite sure what sort of reception you'll receive from them or how much you can rely on their word.

This erratic nature creates a stressful amount of uncertainty and unpredictability. It can leave you walking on eggshells, waiting for the next sudden mood swing or broken promise. Over time, the constant feeling that you never truly know what response you'll get undermines the stability and trust within a relationship. Toxic inconsistency chips away at any sense of safety, making honest communication and teamwork difficult. Instead of being a reliable source of support, their actions force you into a subordinate role where you must anxiously guess their needs at any moment. This type of power imbalance ultimately breeds frustration, resentment and strife between people.

Inconsistency like this is a red flag that there may be deeper emotional problems at the root of a toxic individual's behavior. It pays to be wary of anyone prone to these extremes of unpredictability.

Need for Attention

One hallmark of toxic individuals is an overdependence on receiving attention and support from others without being willing to give as much back. You may notice that they are frequently contacting you through calls, texts, or visits with what seems like minor issues or demands for sympathy. While providing caring for friends in times of need is normal, toxic people take it to an excessive level.

Their needs always take center stage, whether real or imagined, while they neglect to check on your own situation regularly. In conversation, they monopolize the topics and divert discussions back to themselves no matter what is originally brought up. Essentially, they endlessly extract emotional labor and validation from relationships without making equal efforts to support others emotionally in return.

Over time, this one-sided dynamic can leave you feeling drained and unappreciated as if they are not truly interested in also caring for your wellbeing. Attempts to discuss your own problems are often met with deflection, making genuine mutual understanding difficult. While normal to occasionally seek help from loved ones, toxic "attention-seeking" becomes problematic when it forms an engrained pattern of unbalanced taking without proportionate giving within a relationship. Constantly having to reassure someone without receiving it in turn breeds resentment. Excessive dependency on others for attention and emotions is thus a notable sign of deeper toxicity.

Jealousy

While a little jealousy or competitiveness may arise naturally in relationships at times, continuously experiencing these traits from someone else signifies underlying toxic issues. People who are frequently jealous or envious tend to see everything as a contest and everyone else as a threat to their own inflated sense of worth. They feel compelled to constantly compare themselves to others and "one-up" accomplishments, putting others down to elevate their own fragile egos. Beyond being hurtful and insecure behaviors themselves, these actions almost always stem from severe self-centeredness and low self-esteem.

Living with someone who is chronically jealous or competitive will likely involve dealing with subtle and not-so-subtle put-downs, resentment toward your happiness or successes, and attempts to undermine your self-confidence by bringing more attention to their achievements or attributes. They rarely express excitement over your victories without also pointing out how they could have done better. This type of one-sided validation leaves you walking on eggshells, unsure how to celebrate life events without triggering an episode that drains all positivity. Over time, their toxicity eats away at your self-worth through constant comparison and attempts to make everything a rivalry. Learning to spot disproportionate jealousy is key to avoiding getting dragged into its destructive patterns.

Drama

While a bit of playful excitement spices up everyday life at times, some people take drama to an extreme that severely undermines relationships. Toxic individuals have a peculiar attraction to chaos, volatility and heightened emotions. They derive an odd sense of gratification from intentionally inflaming conflicts, escalating minor issues, spreading rumors, and watching interpersonal fires burn out of control. It seems drama and turmoil are the very elements they require to feel entertained or validated.

Whether with friends, partners or family members, these types love stirring the pot by oversharing private stories, making insensitive comments, blaming others unfairly or getting easily offended over petty matters. They then sit back and observe the fallout of anger, tears and disrupted dynamics with what seems like twisted glee. Plans and commitments are constantly put at risk by their impulsive tendencies to unravel situations at any sign of becoming "boring" or stable.

While we've all experienced and learn to manage moments of passion or stress, chronically creating drama takes its toll. It spreads an air of distrust, tension and frayed nerves among all parties. Stable relationships require an ability to resolve issues privately and thoughtfully - not throw fuel on the flames publicly. Those prone to fueling excess chaos should raise concern about deeper motivations that stem from insecurity, control issues or a troubled past.

No Respect for Boundaries

For relationships to thrive, it's essential that all people involved feel comfortable setting reasonable limits and trusting their needs will be respected by others. However, some toxic individuals have difficulty granting even basic autonomy and privacy to those around them. Despite clear communication of boundaries, they feel entitled to constantly violate personal spaces, feelings, and make selfish demands of their time and resources. Whether it's barging in on private conversations, withholding privacy about shared secrets, being too touchy without permission or disrespecting decisions about health/parenting/finances - toxic people justify ignoring clear limits for their own convenience.

Overstepping boundaries whittles away at trust within the relationship. It reveals the toxic person sees others more as possessions they control rather than as independent individuals with their own rights and preferences. They fail to respect personal autonomy or see things from any perspective besides their own. While we all mess up sometimes in relationships, toxic boundary pushers dig in their heels and refuse admittance of wrongdoing. They essentially condition loved ones into feeling they have to justify or get permission for normal actions just to avoid conflicts or retaliation. This created a climate of stress, walking on eggshells and an imbalance of power within interactions over time. Inability to respect clear boundaries should be recognized as a red flag of deeper narcissism and disrespect.

Manipulation

For relationships to be built on a solid foundation of trust, both parties must feel able to be honest and direct with each other without fear of being taken advantage of. Unfortunately, toxic manipulators see others primarily as tools to be exploited for their own gain rather than as human beings deserving respect. They feel entitled to distort facts, withhold information selectively, lie outright, exaggerate stories and play on emotions if it suits their current agenda. The truth and well-being of others matter little in the face of their own wants and needs being met through any means.

Whether twisting your view of shared events, faking excuses to dodge responsibility or lying about their words/actions to coworkers and family, manipulators use their intellect not to strengthen bonds but break them down. They condition loved ones into an anxious state of uncertainty due to not knowing when dishonesty is at play or how to make informed decisions. This calculated influence is not one of care, compromise or teamwork, but of control, power and convenience over others. It poisons goodwill through lost confidence in the foundation that keeps relationships healthy - honesty and transparency between both people. Learning to spot manipulation tactics is vital, as it shows deeper issues like narcissism, lack of empathy and a tendency to objectify others.

Lack of Accountability

In any successful relationship, both parties must be willing to acknowledge when they've made a mistake and take responsibility for their own problematic actions and words and the harm they may have caused. Toxic individuals, however, struggle deeply with this basic concept of accountability. If you bring up something hurtful they said or did, they aren't interested in an earnest discussion or apology. Instead, they deflect, minimize the issue or blame you outright for being too sensitive, misinterpreting their intent or causing their behavior through some perceived past transgression of your own.

Toxic people employ manipulative tactics like gaslighting to manipulate your view of events and make you doubt your own judgment and memories. The sole goal is escaping blame at all costs rather than seeking common ground or a remedy. For toxic individuals, repair and growth through accountability are not priorities in the slightest. Despite any evidence presented, they refuse to validate your experience or feelings. While we all make errors, healthy people own up to problematic impacts rather than stubbornly refusing to learn or change toxic habits for the sake of the relationship. An inability to sincerely accept responsibility when addressed about harm should raise red flags about much deeper issues like narcissism or anti-social traits. Learning to identify lack of accountability is an important first step in avoiding its dysfunctional patterns.

The Difference Between a Bad Day and Toxic Behavior

We've all had our share of bad days where our mood or how we interact with others isn't our best. But most of the time, these incidents are isolated and we're still able to treat people with basic decency and respect. So how do we know when someone has crossed the line into toxic behavior that requires addressing versus just having an off day? It can often be a nuanced distinction, but an important one to identify for our own well-being and healthy relationships.

One major factor is frequency - how regularly certain negative behaviors occur. An off day might happen every once in a blue moon when stress or emotions get the better of us. Toxicity, on the other hand, entails patterns of words and actions that repeatedly undermine a person's well-being over time. If you dread interacting with someone due to consistent insults, manipulations or boundary violations, it's a red flag.

Another distinction lies in intent versus impact. Off days may involve a reaction we later regret, but the root cause was situational rather than a character flaw. Toxicity, however, stems from ingrained traits that prioritize one's own needs and convenience without care for how it affects others. Even if a toxic person doesn't mean direct harm, it's the consistent impact that damages relationships.

Accountability also differs greatly. After a rare outburst, most people will reflect, apologize sincerely and work to improve. Toxic individuals double down with denial, dismissal of others' feelings and refusal to change problematic behaviors. They are threatened by introspection and see relationships as opportunities to extract value rather than contribute equal care, trust and respect.

Excuses are another tell-tale sign - we've all used them on occasion to justify a lapse, but toxicity involves constant blaming of external factors to evade responsibility. Healthy people own their flaws and considerate ways to strengthen close bonds.

Love and familiarity also cloud our vision of toxicity within relationships we're deeply invested in. It's normal to rationalize or forgive repetitive negative behaviors from those closest to us. But when exposure to someone begins feeling like a mental and emotional burden more often than not, it's a red flag.

Toxicity persists regardless of situation while genuine connections ebb and flow with life's ups and downs together. Honing awareness of these contrasts through honest self-reflection helps determine when distance or setting boundaries may be needed for our own well-being, especially if these recognized patterns have persisted despite attempts at discussing concerns and changes. Prioritizing healthy relationships requires acknowledging when behavior stop simply being an "off day." With practice, it gets easier to identify and untangle ourselves from the complexities of toxicity for good.

Identifying Toxicity in Close Relationships

Love has a remarkable ability to cloud our vision and skew our perception of realities that might otherwise be unavoidably clear. This is especially problematic when it comes to identifying toxicity in our closest relationships where deep affection and shared history color how we interact and view each other's actions. However, it's important that we make an effort to overcome love's blinding effects for the sake of our own well-being and health.

Toxic patterns can seep into relationships with loved ones very gradually over time. Subtle early signs may be regularly dismissed or normalized due to emotions and familiarity breeding blindness. This is often the case with family where undesirable behaviors have become so entrenched throughout childhood that we don't recognize their effect until gaining perspective as independent adults. Toxic parents, in particular, can insidiously undermine our sense of self-worth and security from a young age through control, criticism or other dysfunctions.

While toxicity also damages bonds with lifelong friends, it may be even harder to identify due to not having the same natural guard that family ties instill. When toxicity emerges later in life following a friend's poor involvement with toxic partners or ideologies, we overlook warning signs due to wanting to preserve what was once strong. Only major incidents shake our blindness to how far the relationship has deteriorated due to toxic influence over time.

In romantic relationships, lovesickness is perhaps the greatest blindfold of all. Over years, small poor behaviors escalate yet go unaddressed since addressing them risks damage to the idealized notion of unity. Dependency and commitment to vows or children together further lock us into denial even as mental/emotional abuse takes root. Only outside perspective or a damaging incident shatters illusions to expose the depth of toxicity accepted for too long.

To overcome love's blindness, we must be willing to acknowledge hard truths with courage and care for our own well-being above all else. Have frank discussions with trusted confidants to gain insight into interactions we're blind to see clearly. Be open to respectful criticism of our dynamic and how it affects us without defensiveness. Challenge habitual rationalizations and make room for the possibility of toxicity, however discomforting. Track subtle patterns objectively and set boundaries where disrespect emerges to prevent further damage. Consider counseling to untangle damage done and determine a healthy path forward, even if that means difficult changes for the relationship.

Let's take a look at three specific relationships and how you can spot the most subtle signs of toxic behavior. Remember that some points may apply to all of your closest relationships.

Toxic Behavior from Family

Families can be some of the most formative relationships in our lives, but their dysfunctions are also prone to slipping under the radar. While overt abuse leaves scars, more subtle toxic patterns risk being normalized and thus even more damaging long-term to mental health and well-being. It's important to develop awareness of these covert signs so we can establish necessary boundaries for a balanced life.

One subtle yet concerning signal is constantly feeling like you're walking on eggshells around certain family members. Interactions are filled with anxiety, tiptoeing to avoid flare-ups and feeling judged. Arguments regularly turn personal and make it "us against them." Healthy debates don't put people on the defensive or leave hurt feelings.

Individuality not being accepted is another red flag - this includes sexuality, religious/political beliefs, relationship/parenting choices or opinions diverging from expectations without being respected. Toxic families see themselves as authority figures and expect compliance to traditional roles rather than supporting self-discovery.

Using disapproval as an unspoken control tactic also harms well-being and independence. Living only for another's fluctuating approval breeds low self-esteem. Similarly, frequent unmet expectations from family plant seeds of resentment and disappointment in relationships meant to be a safe harbor.

Subtle domination through micro-managing and intrusive parenting of adult children/grandchildren shows lack of trust in others' decision-making abilities and independence. Overstepping reasonable boundaries chips away at feelings of autonomy over time within supposedly supportive networks.

While direct abuse leaves scars, the erosion caused by subtle toxicity can be just as scarring long-term and harder to place a finger on due to normalization. Recognizing when relationships meant for support feel more like a liability is key. While continuing connections, establishing space for well-being through setting firmer limitations if needed helps restore empowerment within even complex family dynamics. Our right to overall mental peace and independence deserves protecting for optimal quality of life.

Toxic Friends

Friendships are meant to enrich our lives through fun, trust, and mutual understanding. However, some bonds may covertly do more harm than good over time by disguising toxicity as care. It's important to recognize warning signs that indicate when a relationship's costs may be outweighing its benefits.

Reliability issues like chronic flakiness with plans without valid excuses or failing to be present for important events breeds resentment and casts doubt on how much the friendship truly matters to that person. Feeling emotionally drained more often than uplifted after socializing with someone rather than energized from quality time also speaks volumes.

Excessive negativity seeping into interactions through frequent aggressive insults disguised as "just joking" or hurtful gossip spreads an overall gloom that contradicts friendship's purpose. Chronic moodiness without accountability that dumps stress onto others is unfair.

Crossing physical boundaries warrants concern too - whether it's drunken belligerence, unwanted touching or consistently invading personal spaces. Disrespecting limits diminishes trust over time.

Guilt trips for pursuing one's own interests instead of prioritizing the toxic friend's every demand breeds codependency rather than interdependence. Healthy support allows individuality.

Failing to express basic gratitude also leaves an imbalance - friendships thrive when both parties feel appreciated for their contributions rather than taken for granted.

While confronting friends requires tact, disregarding concerning patterns risks long-term effects on mental well-being. Addressing issues and establishing boundaries if unheeded helps restore equilibrium. Toxic traits stemming from unmanaged personal problems may unfortunately mean distancing is healthier long-term for all parties involved. Self-care necessitates limiting exposure to consistently draining influences posing as friends.

Toxic Romances

Healthy romantic partnerships provide unconditional acceptance, open communication, trust and personal growth for both individuals over time. However, subtle yet corrosive toxicity can inhibit relationships from meeting basic needs and flourishing if problematic behaviors go unaddressed.

Constant bickering, resentment and difficulty engaging tenderly are red flags, as quality interactions are a relationship's foundation. Lack of mutual emotional support also damages intimacy and balance.

Possessiveness through jealousy and attempts to dominate/isolate from loved ones chip away at autonomy essential for well-being. Partners should complement each other's lives, not demand full ownership of them.

Major unilateral financial decisions without discussion reflect imbalance rather than teamwork between individuals building a life together. Similar issues arise if personal responsibilities or decision-making are unfairly shouldered by only one side.

Failure to care for oneself physically or mentally within the relationship signals codependency rather than interdependence. Prioritizing personal growth alongside a partnership is equally important.

Making excuses to avoid time with one's partner represents a more profound issue requiring honest reflection instead of indefinite endurance hoping for spontaneous change.

Toxic behaviors like ridiculing in front of others or abusing trust through lies create traumatic associations rather than feeling secure and uplifted within the bond over the long run.

While addressing issues requires sensitivity, ignoring problematic patterns risks far greater costs to well-being and the viability of the relationship down the line. Conversations to establish healthier dynamics and set boundaries if needed can restore healthier foundations for the partnership to grow on. Self-reflection also helps discern deep-seated toxicity versus issues couples can work through jointly for mutual benefit. With effort, problematic interactions are not inevitable - but willingness from both partners is key.

Why We Hold On to Toxic Relationships

We've all felt trapped in a relationship that just isn't working anymore. Whether it's a friend, family member, or romantic partner, sometimes we hold on long after we should have let go.

Among friends, toxicity often stems from an imbalance of power or one-sidedness. One friend may seek to control the other through manipulation, insulting jokes taken too far, or only contacting when they want something. Over time, the targeted friend loses their sense of agency and self-worth in the relationship. They begin conceding to unhealthy demands out of worn-down willpower. The toll on mental health can be devastating - social isolation, low mood, and trust issues are common outcomes as the victim questions their value without their toxic "friend's" approval.

In family relationships, abuse is sometimes dismissed as "that's just how they are." But a toxic parent or sibling uses the same control tactics as other abusers - minimizing valid concerns ("you're being too sensitive"), gaslighting realities ("I never said that"), and exploitative behaviors with no regard for consent or boundaries. Their victim endures invisible scars as normal meter breaks from constantly walking on eggshells. Depression and anxiety disorders frequently emerge from an inability to relax in what should be a safe haven.

The workplace harbors toxicity when a manager regularly demeans subordinates, takes credit for their work or fosters an atmosphere of fear and competition. Over time, productivity declines as employees focus energy on survival rather managing real responsibilities. Physical health problems often accompany the chronic stress as blood pressure rises and immunity weakens. Victims begin self-medicating with substances or avoiding work entirely through frequent sick days.

And of course, romantic relationships leave some of the deepest wounds when they degrade into abuse. Gaslighting, insults, control and isolation chip away at identity until victims lose sense of what they want or deserve. Post-traumatic stress symptoms emerge as hypervigilance and flashbacks to past hurt resurface for years after leaving. Self-esteem crumbles from internalizing lies that "no one else will want you."

So why is it that we stay connected to people who treat us badly? There are a few key reasons we tend to get stuck in toxic situations.

One major contributor is familiarity. Even if a relationship brings us more pain than joy these days, the abuse feels familiar - like an old pair of shoes that may be falling apart but are comfortable in their own way. We convince ourselves that it's not so bad and it's easy to settle for "the devil you know" rather than facing the unknown of changing things up. On some deep level we've grown accustomed to the toxicity, and moving on requires stepping out of our comfort zone which can seem scary to many.

Fear of being alone or letting someone down also plays a role. We tell ourselves it would be selfish to remove this person from our lives, even if all they do is take from us emotionally. Or we feel insecure that we won't find someone else to fill their place if we separate. These fears can paralyze us into staying rather than exploring healthier alternatives that may feel risky in comparison.

Low self-esteem contributes to staying as well. Over time, abusive relationships slowly chip away at our self-worth until we begin to feel unworthy of respect and kindness. We normalize mistreatment and come to see it as what we deserve. When self-esteem is low, it's easy to believe the nasty things a toxic person says rather than trusting in our own value.

Hope is another factor - the hope that with enough patience and understanding on our part, the other person will change their hurtful ways. We cling to promises to do better in the future, only to be disappointed again and again. But ending the cycle fully requires letting go of unrealistic hopes and accepting people for who they are, not who we want them to become.

We also hesitate to disappoint loved ones who want us to patch things up. Friends and family likely see the good in the person that's been lost over time, and we don't want to sever the connection they still value. But at the end of the day, we have to prioritize our own well-being over keeping others content with the status quo.

The truth is, no one is perfect and every relationship requires work. But some connections simply drain our life force while providing little in return. When the costs of staying attached start outweighing any benefits, it's time to value our own mental health and walk away. Easier said than done - healing from toxic ties requires courage, self-reflection and support from those who respect our needs. Still, our worth isn't defined by anyone else's approval. With persistence, we can break free.

Insecurity, Attraction, and Fear

When people find themselves trapped in dysfunctional relationships, one of the first questions they inevitably face is "why do you stay?" From abusive spouses to toxic friend groups, outsiders often assume there must be an obvious tipping point where one simply walks away. But as any victim knows, the reality is far more complex, with rationality clouded by powerful undercurrents pulling them back into harm's way time and again.

To heal, we must shine a light on the core drivers keeping us tethered - even when our well-being demands cutting the cord. Insecurity, attraction, and fear form an insidious trifecta that justifies mistreatment and delays escape. On the surface, excuses like "they aren't that bad" or "I don't have other options" soothe the emotional wounds. But these are mere Band-Aids obscuring festering issues needing real diagnosis and treatment if we want to break free long-term.

Insecurity lies at the heart for many. Whether low self-esteem seeking validation or anxiety around uncertainty, clinging to what's familiar provides temporary comfort despite toxicity. As social creatures, habit and routine comfort us even if storms rage inside. On a primitive level, it makes evolutionary sense to endure hardship with known prospects rather than risk death striking in the unfamiliar. However, we have evolved past such limiting instincts - we can and will survive independence, gaining a life without someone else defining our worth.

In my own past, insecurity featured heavily. Ex-partners exploited questioning aspects of my identity and role, betting I'd rather endure mistreatment than solitude. Moving in too fast tied me to one, while another convinced small financial slights weren't intentionally harmful. Both gambled my fear of effort would deter ending things, even as the relationships soured. Breaking free allowed developing routines respecting my values, proving insecurity's lies as self-fulfilling prophecies released their power.

Attraction, another anchor, blinds us to red flags through rose-colored glasses. While a beautiful thing binding compatible souls, intense attraction leaves one vulnerable if the object is unkind or manipulative beneath the surface charm. Love, the saying goes, is indeed blind - and abusers bank on this, altering once an individual is hooked. Furthermore, attraction transcends sexuality; intense bonds to family, ideologies or idols elicit similar vulnerability to influence.

For me, attraction blinded views of exes' unacceptable behaviors as they shifted tactics. Their initial appeal led accepting flaws as surmountable bumps rather than incompatibility warning signs. Only diversifying close connections revealed unhealthy dependence and gave space to see clearly again. While attraction itself is natural, toxic ties leverage this to circumvent boundaries and delay parting ways even as mistreatment chips away at well-being.

Fear of change, of disappointment and of the unknown likewise paralyzes many with cold feet about leaving. Phantom scenarios of survival difficulties abroad paralyze when compared to familiar misery at home. However couragefully facing fears proves them less formidable than imagined - as I discovered in my breaks from exes, where calm replaced chaos and strength emerged from within rather than another.

Ultimately, facing excuses' underlying drivers with compassion empowers recognizing one's value beyond another's whims. Insecurity, attraction and fear are human - but using awareness to overcome rather than excuse harm keeps integrity intact. With support, alleged shortcomings transmute to strengths, and liberty is claimed. Though the road is long, life awaits those journeying on to better destinations and connections ahead.

We've all got our reasons for sticking around, but sometimes those reasons are more like excuses. Let's break them down and see why they're not doing us any favors.

"They aren't really like that." – Oh, this old excuse. It's like we're trying to convince ourselves we're dating Jekyll, not Hyde. But here's the thing: if they're showing you a side that's hurtful or toxic, that's part of who they are. It's not a costume they put on for fun. You wouldn't say, "The sky isn't really blue" just because it's sometimes grey or orange, right? People are the sum of all their behaviors, not just the good ones.

"I don't have another option." – This is a tough one, because it can feel so real. But let's be honest - is being with someone who makes you miserable really better than being on your own? It's like saying you'd rather eat moldy bread than no bread at all. You always

have options, even if they're not obvious right now. Being single might feel scary, but it's also an opportunity to grow and find someone who truly values you.

"They never hit me." – Whoa there, let's not set the bar so low it's underground! Physical abuse isn't the only kind of abuse. Emotional and verbal abuse can leave scars you can't see but that hurt just as much. It's like saying, "Well, they never set me on fire" - that's not exactly a ringing endorsement, is it? You deserve to feel safe and respected in all ways, not just physically.

"It's the community aspect I'd miss." – I get it, losing friends or a social circle can be tough. But if these people only come as a package deal with someone who's toxic for you, are they really your friends? It's like staying at a party where the music's too loud and the food's gone bad just because you're worried about FOMO. There's a whole world out there full of new communities waiting to welcome you.

"I don't want to hurt them." – This one's a real heart-tugger. It shows you're a caring person, which is great! But here's the catch - by staying in a relationship that's not working, you're hurting both of you in the long run. It's like holding onto a hot pan because you don't want to drop it and make a mess. Sometimes, you've got to let go to stop the pain.

"They offer me something amazing, something I can't find anywhere else." – Ah, the golden handcuffs. Sure, maybe they're the only one who gets your obscure movie references or makes that special pasta sauce you love. But is that worth the price of your happiness and well-being? It's like keeping a pair of shoes that give you blisters just because they're a limited edition. There are 7 billion people on this planet - I bet you can find someone else who watches cult classics and knows their way around a kitchen.

"I take the good days with the bad." – Life's all about balance, right? But if you're constantly walking on eggshells, waiting for the next "bad day" to hit, that's not balance - that's living in fear. It's like saying you enjoy rollercoasters because the slow climb up is so peaceful, ignoring the terrifying drop that follows. In a healthy relationship, the good should far outweigh the bad.

"It's not their fault, they are just mentally ill." – Mental health is important, and it's good that you're compassionate. But here's the thing: mental illness might explain behavior, but it doesn't excuse it. If someone's not taking steps to manage their condition and it's hurting you, that's a problem. It's like saying it's okay for someone to keep crashing into your car because they refuse to wear their glasses. You can be understanding without being a punching bag.

"I have to think of others before myself."Selflessness is admirable, but martyr syndrome? Not so much. You can't pour from an empty cup, as they say. If you're constantly putting everyone else's needs before your own, you'll end up drained and resentful. It's like being on a plane and giving your oxygen mask to everyone else first - you'll pass out before you can help anyone.

Remember, you deserve a relationship that lifts you up, not one that constantly knocks you down. It's okay to prioritize your own well-being. In fact, it's necessary. Don't let these justifications keep you stuck in a situation that's hurting you. You've got one life - make it a good one, surrounded by people who truly care about you.

Unpacking the Roots of Toxic Relationships

Fear forms a powerful undercurrent in toxic relationships, exploiting our instincts for survival against better judgment. But fear itself serves natural purposes - alerting us to real dangers so we act cautiously. In dysfunctional bonds, manipulators hijack fear responses for control instead.

To break free long-term, we need to understand where fears come from so their power can fade.

One thing that keeps us afraid is worrying what will happen without the other person. When a relationship is all we know, being alone into the future seems really scary. But our lives won't fall apart like we imagine - we survived before and will survive after, even stronger having faced this challenge. Others in your shoes did it too.

Another fear is what the toxic person might do back, like revenge or saying bad things about us to mutual friends. Abusers worked hard training us to be on edge, so it's normal to feel on guard. But their threats aim to control - contacting authorities protects us if needed while getting far away. Their actions aren't our problem anymore either.

Not wanting to disappoint family or peers stuck in the past also feels stressful. But we didn't choose this life just for appearances - our needs matter most in the end once we accept not everyone will agree. With practice, confidence grows in our right to happiness.

I was super afraid of all these things leaving exes. I pictured loneliness or them spreading rumors, and felt ashamed others would judge my choices. Once separated though, life continued as before except much lighter without anxiety hanging over me. Police helped enforce no contact, as counseling did processing challenging emotions.

Money or time already invested in the relationship also makes some hesitant to pull the plug, feeling it all needs redeeming somehow. Yet nothing changes bad patterns or brings back lost opportunities - staying just means throwing good moments after bad. We must accept imperfect outcomes then set healthy new goals.

Really taking time to think through held-back worries helps defuse their intensity. Doubts sneak in whenever we feel unsafe or uncertain. But recalling past resilience reminds us of ability to face this too, one step at a time, around people who lift us up instead of weighing us down. Change brings discomfort, yet staying miserable pleases no one in the end - least of all ourselves.

So if you find yourself gripped by fears putting off the exit, know it's normal after trauma bonding warps perceptions of risks.

Identifying Excuses

It can be tough to spot the real reasons we make excuses to linger where we're mistreated. Our unhealthy motivations surface in unique ways based on our personalities and relationship details. The longer abuse goes on, the more elaborate justifications feel too.

But take a step back from emotions clouding judgment. At their core, excuses all connect back to feeling insecure without the toxic tie, strong attachment despite flaws, or aversions to uncertainty.

If we feel inadequate alone and constantly question our worth, insecurity rules us. Clinging for some sense of control fuels denial over inconsistencies. Extreme attraction blurs reality when admiration hijacks willpower. We minimize or justify poor behavior hoping to reclaim "the one" despite evidence being misled all along. Fear holds us hostage as worries overwhelm logic. Thinking only in worst case "what ifs" immobilizes from taking back freedom.

Notice anxious, clingy or volatile behaviors emerging in yourself or the other person meant to disrupt independence. Interrogate patterns of manipulation weaving through excuses like hidden strings.

Let's have a look again at the common excuses given earlier this chapter:

"They aren't really like that."

Saying another person "isn't usually like this" after they acted out or were abusive is a common excuse people use to justify staying in toxic relationships. On the surface it seems reasonable, but when you examine it further it becomes clear why it's misleading.

The phrase implies that person's bad behavior should be forgiven or overlooked because it's supposedly not typical for their character. But does one outburst or moment of anger truly undo a pattern of toxic words and actions? Likely not. Even if a moment was provoked, it still reveals unhealthy tendencies someone needs to work on, not be excused from.

Using this line also suggests the person can change their ways if given another chance. But more often than not, they continue the mistreatment while being "held accountable" for past actions with empty promises of doing better next time. Making excuses like this allows toxic patterns to persist rather than address problems at their root.

Saying it also comes from a place of fear deep down. Admitting the reality of someone's cruelty opens us up to dealing with pain and disappointment, which feels scary. It's easier in the short term to justify away unpleasant truths that upend what we want to believe about a relationship or ourselves.

For those experiencing abuse, the statement serves to protect the other party at their own expense. It delays leaving a situation that threatens well-being. By rationalizing unacceptable behavior as abnormal rather than facing the choice to accept or not accept it, we deny agency over a toxic tie weighing us down.

"I don't have another option."

Saying "I don't have another option" to justify staying in an unhealthy relationship downplays how there are always alternatives, even if they're imperfect or scary. This statement comes from a place of insecurity rather than facing reality.

When someone claims no other choice exists, what they really mean is the potential options induce fear or anxiety. Whether it's insecurity about being lonely, struggling financially, or adjusting to change, leaving the familiar for the unknown triggers worries about survival or failure. But these fears often outweigh realistically assessing other doors that may lead to happier, healthier spots down the road.

Abusers work hard to cut victims off from support systems and chip away at self-esteem until they truly feel stuck without the toxic tie to lean on. But this is an illusion - there are always alternatives, even if they require courage and flexibility to explore. Having the bare minimum of shelter and basic needs met is better than long-term damage from staying stuck.

Saying no other path exists also comes from a place of extreme attraction denying red flags. While no one is perfect, this excuse overlooks how compromise doesn't require tolerating toxicity or losing sense of self-worth simply for meeting some superficial needs superficially. People find fulfillment through many venues beyond whatever binds them to harm despite their better judgment.

Ultimately, this statement prevents taking responsibility to improve circumstances through available if imperfect choices.

"It's not their fault, they are just mentally ill."

Claiming bad behavior stems from a mental illness outside someone's control is an excuse that prevents holding them accountable for their actions and the impact it has. While mental health issues deserve compassion, they don't negate treating others poorly or excuse toxicity.

Saying this comes from a place of wanting to believe the best in people we're attached to, even when reality shows otherwise. There's an element of fear that admitting the truth makes the situation worse somehow. If we acknowledge unacceptable behavior, it opens us up to pain, disappointment and having our perception of the relationship shattered. It's easier in the short term to blame problems on things beyond volition.

There's also a fear that others may reject or negatively judge the toxic person if they truly recognized the dynamics for what they are. This line of thinking comes from a place of prioritizing their comfort and image over our own well-being. But we teach people how to treat us - calling out problems with empathy and boundaries is caring enough to want positive growth, not condemnation.

Regardless of mental health factors, we each have a responsibility for our own behaviors and how they affect others. While support exists for managing conditions, it doesn't negate damaging actions or shift accountability. Staying exposes ourselves to harm waiting for unlikely change that may never come at our expense.

Ultimately this excuse prevents clearly seeing an unhealthy situation for what it is - a barrier against honesty needed to improve circumstances or remove ourselves from danger. Mental illnesses call for treatment, not excuses reinforcing dysfunction or toxicity just to avoid hard truths.

"I have to think of others before myself."

Saying that they must prioritize others over their own well-being is an excuse that prevents protecting themselves from toxic situations. While caring for loved ones is important, using this logic to justify abuse diminishes their personal worth and needs.

On the surface, it seems selfless to endure hardship so family or peers aren't inconvenienced by relationship changes. But this mindset comes from a place of deep insecurity and fear of being alone through difficult times. It refuses to acknowledge how witnessing toxicity negatively impacts others as well in the long run. Children Learning unhealthy patterns by thinking abuse is normal or relationships are meant to cause pain and distress. Coworkers exposed to spillover from volatile dynamics. Friends concerned but unsure how to help without overstepping. By dismissing one's own suffering, these impact are minimized rather than addressed for all's wellbeing.

Toxic bonds prioritize superficial optics of "keeping the peace" over substance, safety and empowering independence. But self-care ensures best ability to support networks too. Staying exposes weaknesses others can exploit while valuing propriety over stability.

Ultimately this excuse prevents taking responsibility for one's circumstances and self-worth and puts others in caretaking roles they aren't equipped for.

As we've explored, there are many justifications people use to rationalize staying in unhealthy bonds against their better judgment. But at their core, excuses ultimately connect back to fears of insecurity, attraction blinding reality, and the uncertainties change represents.

Admitting the truth means facing uncomfortable wounds and disrupted perceptions of a relationship. It's easier in the short term to soothe painful emotions through justification rather than risk uncomfortableness. But this approach just delays facing problems for honest resolution or exit when improvement isn't realistic.

Toxic relationships prioritize superficial satisfaction of fears over genuine well-being through manipulation of insecurities till one's worth depends on another's whims. This prevents responsibility for circumstances and self-care in favor of resigned acceptance of dysfunction. But we each deserve stability founded on honest assessment of suitability rather than distorted hopes clinging to sunk costs. No connection is perfect, yet compromise requires mutual care, trust and respect - not lowering standards simply to avoid fears.

By addressing core psychological roots fueling excuses with empathy and outside perspective, their power dissipates. Independence proves worries false through renewed strength facing uncertainty. Ultimately, justifications serve short-term coping, not long-term healing from dysfunction's scars.

Take Responsibility For Your Own Well-Being

At some point in our lives, we've all put others' needs above our own. Whether it's staying late at work to help a coworker in need or lending money to a friend who promises they'll pay you back, most of us are willing to sacrifice our time and resources to support those around us from time to time. And there's nothing wrong with showing a little compassion now and then.

However, taking care of others cannot come at the expense of neglecting your own wellbeing. Continually putting others first without tending to your own needs will only leave you depleted and unable to be there for anyone in the long run. This is a trap many find themselves stuck in when it comes to toxic relationships. So how do you avoid letting toxicity drain you while still maintaining your caring nature? The key is learning when to say "no" and prioritizing self-care. Easier said than done, I know, but with practice it gets easier to stick up for yourself without feeling selfish.

Let's start with understanding why it's so hard to look out for number one when toxicity creeps in. Many of us grew up being taught that it's impolite or uncaring to refuse a request. We don't want to disappoint or upset others, even if fulfilling their demand would negatively impact us. Additionally, toxic relationships rely on manipulating our helpful nature - they bank on us caving to avoid conflict.

Over time, constantly giving in takes a massive emotional and physical toll. You begin to lose touch with your own wants, needs and boundaries as focusing externally becomes habit. Sound familiar? This pattern leaves you vulnerable to being drained and used. And how can you possibly help others from an empty cup?

The key is shifting your mindset from "How can I please this person?" to "What do I need to feel okay?" Start small by scheduling time for yourself, whether it's an afternoon walk, dinner with friends or hobby time. This helps fill your cup back up so you can engage from a place of fullness rather than scarcity. From there, get comfortable saying "no" politely yet firmly when requests cross your boundaries. Phrases like "That doesn't work for me right now, but let me know if another option comes up" remove the guilt factor. You don't owe endless justification - a simple "No, thank you" will do. With practice, it gets easier to stick up for yourself respectfully.

When toxicity seeps in despite your best efforts, it's time for some tough love. Set boundaries and consistently enforce consequences when they're crossed. Maybe it's limiting contact until an apology is given or ending the relationship if abuse persists. Your wellbeing deserves protection even if others don't agree.

The truth is, you can't pour from an empty cup. Caring for yourself - mentally, emotionally and physically - is how you maintain the capacity to show up fully for others. It's not selfishness but self-preservation. With patience and consistency, you can reclaim your power in toxic relationships and feel good doing so. Just don't forget to take care of yourself along the way.

Valuing Yourself

Relying entirely on others to look out for your wellbeing in toxic situations often does more harm than good. While friends and loved ones want to help, making them solely responsible for your protection creates an unhealthy codependency that burns them out over time. It also prevents you from developing the independence and self- assurance needed to stand up for yourself down the line.

The sad truth is that no one, no matter how caring, can shield you from toxicity forever. At some point, you'll likely encounter difficult people when support isn't immediately available. So learning to spot red flags and protecting your own interests is an important survival skill. However, defending your boundaries first requires truly valuing who you are and what you deserve.

Easier said than done if past toxic experiences have eroded your self-worth. Narcissists, abusers and other difficult personalities thrive on making their targets question themselves. Through gaslighting, insults and control tactics, they aim to elevate their importance while convincing victims they're "undeserving." Over time, this type of manipulation can leave deep wounds, making it hard to recognize your inherent worth.

So how do you rebuild when toxicity has you doubting your value?

- Start small with daily affirmations - look in the mirror and list qualities you appreciate about yourself, from your kindness to your work ethic.

- Nurture relationships with people who respect you instead of tear you down. Make time for hobbies you find meaningful to remind yourself life isn't all about others' opinions.

- Validate your thoughts, feelings and needs instead of dismissing them. You deserve to have boundaries respected just like anyone else.

- With compassion, reflect on experiences from your perspective to gain clarity - then choose to leave the past in the past. While scars remain, you determine the power the toxic relationship has over you.

- As self-belief strengthens, standing up to toxicity gets easier. You recognize disrespect and refuse to internalize it. Instead of staying silent to avoid conflict, honest communication from a place of worthiness sets expectations.

- And if toxicity persists, you confidently remove it from your life without guilt.

Nobody should face difficult people alone. But by valuing yourself instead of relying entirely on the protection of others, you gain independence and the strength to set healthy limits. With time and effort, former victims can become survivors empowered in even the most toxic environments - not by changing themselves, but by changing their perspective on who they've always been. Your worth isn't defined by the opinions of a select few; it's an inherent human right.

Overcoming the Toxicity

Being trapped in an abusive situation is traumatizing in ways often misunderstood until experienced firsthand. When your sense of safety and control have been stripped away, it's a natural human response to bond with your captor for survival - even if they're the source of torment. This psychological phenomenon known as Stockholm Syndrome demonstrates just how deeply toxicity can disrupt normal thinking and fracture a person's core.

While the immediate environment determines whetherStockholm Syndrome manifests, escaping an abusive dynamic doesn't automatically undo the damage. Former victims routinely feel disoriented and confused as they try to rediscover who they are independent of their toxic past. With identity and self-assurance dismantled piece by piece, regaining solid ground is an uphill battle riddled with lingering effects.

Post-traumatic stress also ensures everyday reminders, however innocuous, trigger panic associated with past trauma. Completely normal behaviors like asserting boundaries or prioritizing your needs now induce fear conditioned by toxicity. It's easy to label these healthy actions as "toxic" themselves due to induced discomfort.

Healing requires recognizing trauma's continued influence doesn't invalidate your worth or reality. You survived the unsurvivable - that strength endures within you regardless of how buried beneath layers of pain. With compassion, acknowledge trauma's fingerprints without letting them define you or determine your potential.

Rebuilding identity and self-esteem necessitate daily affirmations to rewire negative core beliefs. Look within and appreciate qualities having nothing to do with past judgments. Nourish relationships reinforcing your intrinsic value rather than what you can provide others.

Validate emotions instead of dismissing uncomfortable ones sparked by triggers. Their emergence shows trauma speaking, not personal weakness - sit with discomfort as it lessens over time. Journaling exercises perspective by reflecting how you'd encourage a loved one, not how trauma conditions you to internalize blame.

Set boundaries not from a place of fear but of empowerment and care for self. Toxic teachings aimed dismantling agency; retake control by making choices aligning with your wellbeing. Defend limits with compassion, understanding others aren't obligated understanding yours.

Accepting flaws doesn't require abandoning self-respect. Toxicity thrives on convincing victims they're unworthy; counteract that lie by consciously extending yourself the same compassion you would a friend. You survived the unsurvivable - that strength remains and your worth was never defined by those aiming to diminish it. Keep moving forward.